*Complayntes for
Doctor Neuro*
& other poems

Also by John Matthias

Poetry
Bucyrus (1970)
Turns (1975)
Crossing (1979)
Bathory & Lermontov (1980)
Northern Summer (1984)
A Gathering of Ways (1991)
Swimming at Midnight (1995)
Beltane at Aphelion (1995)
Pages: New Poems & Cuttings (2000)
Working Progress, Working Title (2002)
Swell & Variations on the Song of Songs (2003)
New Selected Poems (2004)
Kedging (2007)
Trigons (2010) *
Collected Shorter Poems, Vol. 2 (2011) *
Collected Longer Poems (2012) *
Collected Shorter Poems, Vol. 1 (2013) *

Translations
Contemporary Swedish Poetry (1980) (with Göran Printz-Påhlson)
Jan Östergren: Rainmaker (1983) (with Göran Printz-Påhlson)
The Battle of Kosovo (1987) (with Vladeta Vučković)
Three-Toed Gull: Selected Poems of Jesper Svenbro (2003)
                                        (with Lars-Håkan Svensson)

Essays
Reading Old Friends (1992)
Who Was Cousin Alice? and Other Questions (2011) *
At Large (2016) *

Editions
23 Modern British Poets (1971)
Introducing David Jones (1980)
David Jones: Man and Poet (1989)
Selected Works of David Jones (1992)
Notre Dame Review: The First Ten Years (2009) (with William O'Rourke)

(* indicates a Shearsman publication)

John Matthias

Complayntes for Doctor Neuro
& other poems

Shearsman Books

First published in the United Kingdom in 2016 by
Shearsman Books
50 Westons Hill Drive
Emersons Green
BRISTOL
BS16 7DF

Shearsman Books Ltd Registered Office
30–31 St. James Place, Mangotsfield, Bristol BS16 9JB
(this address not for correspondence)

www.shearsman.com

ISBN 978-1-84861-518-2

ACKNOWLEDGEMENTS
My thanks the editors of the following journals and anthologies for printing
some of the poems in this book:

The Arts of Peace: An Anthology: 'Anniversary.'
Boulevard: 'Yeats, Pound and Pooh: Stone Cottage, Sussex'; 'The
Doppelgänger's Hands'; 'Tourist Guide to Crete.'
The Common: 'Post-Colonial Chicken.'
Gods and Mortals: Modern Poems on Classical Myths: 'Icarus.'
Long Poem Magazine: 'The M's's.'
The New Yorker: 'The House of Headache.'
Parnassus: 'Some Histories.'
Poetry: 'After Las Formas Puras, after Lorca'; 'After Quevedo.'
Salmagundi: 'Refusing an Archive'; 'Notes of an Uninvited Guest.'
Stand: 'I didn't, I won't'; 'Some Histories.'

In different forms, these poems appeared as performance pieces in my book
Six Short Plays (BlazeVox, 2016): 'Post-Colonial Chicken,'
'Three Act Play,' and 'The M's's.'

My thanks also to early readers of these poems: Robert Archambeau, Michael
Anania, Peter Michelson, Herbert Leibowitz, Stephen Fredman, and Vincent
Sherry. And thanks to Katie Lehman for help in preparing the manuscript.

Contents

Dedication: *Of Artemis Aging . . .*   7

I

Some Histories   11
Pending a Piano Player: Maurice Ravel's *Gaspard de la Nuit*   12
Anniversary   13
Refusing an Archive   14
The Doppelgänger's Hands   15
Yeats, Pound and Pooh: Stone Cottage, Sussex   16
On the (Unfinished) Beach   17
Notes of an Uninvited Guest   18
In *Skunk Hour*'s Maine: Reunion at the Fosse   19
Paddy's Broken Road   21
Elegy for Seamus Heaney   22

II

From *Senile Sextets*   25
Song of the Association's Spokesman   26
Who Lives at the P.O.?   27
Proof   28
I Didn't, I Won't   29
Post-Anecdotal (with a New Third Part)   31
Tourist Guide to Crete   33
A Hard Man Is Good to Find   35
I Copy That   36
Firing Neurons à la Valéry   37
Villon à la Rodefer
A Sinking Boat (2)

III

After *Las Formas Puras,* after Lorca   43
After Quevedo   44
Icarus   45
The House of Headache   46
Two from *Des Petits Hommages*   47
A Backward *Zone*   49
Camilla of the Volscians   52

The Major Odes   57

IV
Three Act Play   63
Postcolonial Chicken   66
The M's's   70
Some Instruments for Mr. Frick   79

V
Complayntes for Doctor Neuro   83

Notes   100

Dedication: *Of Artemis, Aging . . .*

for Diana

But of course she does not age! Immortal, she
Does what she has always done: There is no future tense
To drag her down, to soften her hard body,
Compromise her chastity. Through the ages she is
What she always is: There is no past except for those
She touches, touched, will touch: They rise and fall
With time, but she is timeless. Does she envy them
Their human grace to change? Callisto, found with child,
Became a constellation with her son, Arktos, rising up
Behind her in the circumpolar sky. Actaeon turned
Into a stag. I've seen Diana at her bath but never was
Devoured by my hounds, only by my longing.
Young, she moved like the wife of Menelaos in the
Eyes of Telemakhos — *straight as a shaft of gold.*
But even Helen by that time had changed: Hausfrau
In the great Lakedaimon mansion house, she began
To age. The red-haired king found his lady all the more
Amazing and the struggle on the beachhead year by year
Receded in his memory. Vindictive Artemis forgets
Nothing and does not forgive. Her eternal present
Is as sterile as the moon's. If she could change, she
Might be like the woman called by her Roman name
Reading in a book beside the fire in my own house.
She has come down all these years with me, and she
Is getting old. She turns the pages slowly, then looks up.
Her wise ironic glance is *straight as a shaft of gold.*

I

Some Histories

My cat is eating a spider that she clawed
Out of its beautiful web. I do not interfere,
Am not like amber falling on the springtail
Sixteen million years ago that turned up
In a CT scan playing horseback on a mayfly.
My wife's CT scan was negative, and so
We hugged each other walking home from the lab.
Nonetheless my cat continues eating the
Spider and, after that, the fly the spider hoped
To eat, still struggling in its web. Nothing
Was eating at my wife's thymus gland.
A botanist has boasted that he grew a plant
Seeded from some cells preserved in permafrost
For thirty thousand years. In the photograph, it looks
Just like an Easter lily. Hallelujah. DNA has
Risen from the dead. There's a record
Somewhere of a rite in Poland where the villagers,
All bereft of witches, substituted as a sacrifice
A kind of Guy Fawkes effigy stuffed full of cats.
On the pyre, they howled in ungodly ways.
My cat jumps on my lap, purring. In 1574
Federico Barocci painted the Madonna with
An orange tabby reaching for a goldfinch.
From the Hukawng valley, Myanmar, early
Cretaceous period, a tiny fossil holds a wasp
That struggles for its life in etched strands of
Spider silk that caught it ninety million years ago.

Pending a Piano Player:
Maurice Ravel's *Gaspard de la Nuit*

It's hard to play *Gaspard* as from a gibbet
but you're doomed to try. You play the ribs,
the tendons and the nerves. You play
the vertebrae. It's plangent, but *pendu*.
You play erection, which they say is
always part of these executions. Forbidden
love with any mortal woman now, at last
you call upon the nymph Ondine to swim
from the tear rolling from your blinded
eye into the corner of your open mouth.
The audience is stunned: Could it be *grillon*
or *mouche* or *araignée?* Cricket, fly & spider
sing Ondine and Scarbo so that water nymph
and gnome dance together, one on either
pending hand. Every neuromuscular control
is lost. Finger bones fly out into the night.

Anniversary

My wife's father and my own uncle were in it.
It's still that close, that far away.
Millions of lives ago and a tick of geological time.
It's come around again, that day for poppies and
Remembrance. A hundred years this time.
What's a hundred years? What's a hundred
Thousand years? I turn a stone up with my toe
In a Suffolk field where my wife still saw
The horses plowing in her youth, not just in
The poems of Edward Thomas. The stone had
Been waiting for millennia. A man who
Knew three veterans from old Akenfield told me
Of his conversations. In the early days they'd
Take a village full of men together in one company,
Put them in a single trench. One shell left a parish
Destitute. Three alone were only left to tell him.
We wept, one said to him, not because we were
Afraid – we were beyond all fear – but because
We were so dirty, made of the same clay as
The long graves we fought from, lice in our hair
In our eyes, lice all crawling on our balls, and
Cold, cold – like stones in a farmer's frozen field.

Refusing an Archive

Another file of letters in another envelope.
This is like self-burial, heaping earth
upon my own body with a toy spade. Or
getting in a box with all they've asked me for.

They'll even pay for what's too late to use:
my mother's power of attorney, my father's
Living Will. Where is the court in which
I could appeal to leave them void? The doctor's

dead himself who closed my parents' eyes.
And this – charge and counter-charge between
two friends. What was that about? Or connivance
with some Anna? – can't quite make it out –

Emma is it maybe? In the fire with them.
And these! – bad poems. Old, old young poems.
And I should save this corpus? Screw down
the lid on scribblings gasping in a final breath?

The fire, O lucid choir. Sing it into flame.
Flame it into song. Make an archive only
In the Empire of all ash.
Ash the only archive worth an ark at all.

The Doppelgänger's Hands

In the mirror I catch a glimpse of his hands
hanging from my wrists, some other old man's —
dirty, gnarled, arthritic — colder even than
my own, and can't remember, can't understand

where they've been. Or if the left ever knew
what the right one was doing, out in the dark with a spade
digging in his father's grave, looking for things decayed,
all the anger once displayed, the parts that they played?

Or both on his first girl's breasts in a first caress?
Or did they cook his solitary meals, count out his years,
never welcome a single guest, or anybody's kiss?

Did they turn the pages of a thousand books?
All thumbs and knuckles, twisted up in ecstatic fears?
Did they make little fists tighter than this?

Yeats, Pound and Pooh: Stone Cottage, Sussex

> If the poets walked through the woods northeast of the cottage they
> would have crossed the bridge, immortalized by Ernest Shepard on the
> frontispiece to *The House at Pooh Corner*, where Christopher Robin and
> his friends played Pooh-sticks."
> — James Longenbach, *Stone Cottage.*

The poets studied the Japanese Noh, but also
the Yes and Maybe So. It was cold in Sussex and even
a beast could long for the warmth of the hearth
the humans liked, the kindled New Year's fire.
They translated weathers and signs in the terms
The others could understand. They used the words
That came to hand from the muck and the mire.
One of them longed for love, another for fame,
a third for something sweet. And even though
indeed the *winter was icumen in*, not spring,
I like to imagine them one bright hoarfrost day,
Icetree branches click-and-clanging, holding
hands where no birds sang, and walking
all together through the highpine wood and over
Mr. Milne's old bridge, three bears you'd say
of little brain – at least when forced to consider
their worst and most famous thinks – but also each
with a blazing and weirdly magnificent soul,
all three of them left in the lurch by something –
a growing boy, a beautiful woman,
a terrible always and incomprehensible war.

On the (Unfinished) Beach

Crap-shooting Palamedes, beardless, beards
The dumbass Ajax on the beach, bets him lyrics of
A song from *Guys and Dolls* against a Mallarmé.
All's anachronism there, everything's at stake.
Stuck before the walls of Troy for a decade, why
Not make your homo *homo ludens* now and then?
It passes the time. It pesters the rhyme.

The age of heroes dies *right now*. On the beach
For a bitch of a long time. They all get bored.
Some of them are gored by a bull from the sea,
Vicariously dissed and diced. Hands up please who
Know the sum of *ptyx* and *ptyx*. Fish eyes
Taken from the alphabet of wine-dark C's bright gaze
Converting *coup d'état* to *coup de dés*.

Bow before the lady with a blue bow in her hair?
L-Napoléon's sweet whore? Or is it Baudelaire's?
Heir to what the dice said on the beachhead, heir as well
To Damon Runyon tales, farce rolls out again
As tragedy for [. + .] comedians. And they are?
In a throw of the dice: In Palamedes' hand: knuckle-
Bones of nothingness exalt a blather, and unbar . . .

Notes of an Uninvited Guest

High on Molly, he lay on someone's bed;
The rising moon with moonshine
Raised the dead. Much earlier, he thought he'd
(Hand on meth and short of breath)

Outfoxed already raves in Greenwich Village
And outslummed the risen other, who was
Bald and fey and pecker-faced, but tried
To verse him, all defriended, in the hall. Waking

Was a fall into old times, into a kind of
Brick-a-bracky shopping mall, and yet
Domestic. Looking at the shelves he thought,
Pottery makes nothing happen! But has

Anybody tried this groovy stuff? The vendor
Wore a wig and called it snuff.
Thomas was the nominal of normal here,
And bet a bob on Robert, thrust a snout

Into the glitter of the *Geister* . . . Raving
Was the form of greeting among rivals swarming
Reiver modes, "dying of welcome." His little
Hostess thought it queer to leave so early

When he'd only just arrived at *here*. "A stirrup
Cup, no more," he said, and then he trotted off, ahoot,
With the good cop. The bad cop said, "Dearth
Is the matter of Molly. Hands up, with the loot!

Our code book always called you *Parachute*."

In *Skunk Hour*'s Maine: Reunion at the Fosse

Opening the door, I find them swarming
Toward me – all my dead, or
So it seems. But it's just reunion day
And I have been away so long

I'm looking into eyes I haven't seen
For more than forty years. But also
Other eyes. There's Anchises Saul,
Except that it's his son. I poured out

My libation and up came an imposter.
All seemed risen from the dead, sons
And fathers, uncles, nephews,
Aunts, and many who did not come to

The door or even turn around. *Mother,*
I said to someone's back, and when
She turned, she laughed at me. Black sheep
In this family, foreign to this northern shore

I might as well be Robert Lowell caught in
Charlotte's web in Sarah Orne Jewett's
Country of tall pines. My cousin owned
A sailing boat, but I had been the sailor –

Gone so long that no one claimed me
Until now. Had *they* died or had I?
A seeming shade approached,
Then leapt at me with strange embrace:

*We've missed you. You look exactly like
Your father.* I said, *He's dead.* But then
That person took me by the hand and led
Me toward another who came up and

Said: *Neglect! You've neglected all of*
us and yet that hasn't stopped your
Writing. How you've libeled us. What's
The hour that permits the things you've

Done through all these years of
Absence? It isn't this one, nine p.m.
In Maine. It was some petty grievance
That you held against us decades back —

Some lack of understanding, rather.
Everybody wrote against his kin, so
You did too. It was the period style.
It was the period stile, and in you

Pressed your snout. Now look at this.
The vouchsafed vision showed a scene
I've carried with me since my father's
Death, the very afternoon when he

Was buried. Anchises Saul stood
Beside my mother, and my daughter, very
Young and longing for relief from such
A boring day, looked at him and turned to me,

Asking, *Is he's better now?* I asked her: *Who?*
Is grandpa Paul? Not knowing what
To say I looked at Saul. *She thinks I'm Paul.*
No, I said. *He's dead, and this is Saul.*

Paddy's Broken Road

i.m. Patrick Leigh Fermor

"And yet, in another sense, although . . ."
On that fragment the traveller's journal ends.
It might have been that he was slow

Or fast, outpaced his rhythm, stubbed his toe
On time, missed the turning at a bend,
And yet, in another sense, although,

He'd walked from Holland to the rainbow's end
As planned, he felt an emptiness,
And left a fragment only for his friends

Who'd understand his strange and mellow
Grievance – charm his brilliant method to amend –
And yet, in another sense, although . . .

Although he'd write it down, although he might
Restore eventually the light he'd tended,
Now he couldn't see a thing except the night

That lay ahead where every wrong was right.
He'd tried to do what he had first intended.
And yet, in another sense, although . . .
We walk upon an earth we cannot know.

Elegy for Seamus Heaney

Seamus felt it in his feet,
Clods of fuel in the peat.
In the peat a fire to warm
Children not yet even born.

Joseph Brodsky was his friend.
Wystan Auden would amend
Dances William Blake would like,
Tigers lurking in the night.

Metric feet and feet in boots –
Robert Lowell was shown his roots
Welcomed in an Irish town
Where the sky was falling down.

Mister Yeats was dead by then
Honored by some mortal men
Heaney his example took,
Brooding sky and flying rook.

Even Possum shares the beat
In Joseph's poem for Thomas Stearns.
Heaney's poem for Brodsky, dead,
Lives in turns, not Grecian urns.

What dread turning plow or spade
Having dug up things well made
Digs now to inter a shade.
World poets learn your trade!

II

From *Senile Sextets*

Jerry Atrick
Got a hat trick
Skating for the Boston Bruins

No one cares
About old bears
Iced out in their ruins

•

Al T. Zimmer
Saw in a glimmer
A face he thought he'd known

Hewn of stone
It was a clone
Of what he'd had for dinner

•

Grandpa Geezer
Had a seizure
Early in the morn

Couldn't cut it
Though he'd put it
Right up to the porn

Song of the Association's Spokesman

after Carlos Drummond de Andrade

(*for the NRA*)

In the middle of my head there is an hole
there is an hole in the middle of my head
there is an hole
in the middle of my head there is an hole.

I'll never forget my reflection
as I stare at myself in the mirror.
I'll never forget that in the middle of my head
there is an hole
there is an hole in the middle of my head
in the middle of my head there is an hole.

Who Lives at the P.O.?

What? People I've known on postage stamps?
I'm stopped in my tracks, stumped for speech.
Finally I manage "Three out of ten."
The lady behind the counter asks me
"Three out of ten what?" "People I know,
Or knew." "Four dollars fifty," she says.
"For What?" "Four strips of forever poets."
I remember a few conversations, a letter or
Two (stamped with a president's mug), poems
Shared or critiqued. *Hwæt? . . . in gear-dagum?*
"Four dollars and fifty cents," she says.
What's the world coming to? One of these
Postal heads says: "See! Poetry *is* a kind of
Money after all." I'm feeling dizzy, must be
Getting on, one way or another. Now I can imagine
Just about anything, even coins issuing from
Some kind of Poundian mint: the Ashbery dime,
The Hass half dollar, the Pinsky penny.
Just mail your letter, old man. So off they go –
Oh Gwendolyn . . . Joseph . . . Denise.

Proof

Let cancel cancel cancel
John Wilkinson

My proof contains a "grocer's apostrophe,"
I'm told. Not true. It's *it's* that should appear
right where it's at. The "reader" has misread.
Uncopy Copy Editor, you copy that? *Stet stet.*
But then I think apostrophe in all its uses,
right or wrong, is doomed. No more shouts of
longing from the grocer: "O lovely lettuce heads,
radishes and mangel-wurzels! O stalky celery
and Brussels sprouts!" Journalist apprentices, neo-
phyte professors, tyro poets, bebop pamphleteers,
all dispense with them, usage manuals in the dust.
Milton, thou should'st be with us at this hour!
Even I, proponent of an endgame preposition
got this proof's contraction right. But *'s's* at an
impasse, hours ticking down the time until we may
be tickled by the rub of love possessing nothing but
its finger pointing not at grocer's claim and elegy
for ownership but just at Gertrude's no *there* there
for which they're all to prove their penny's worth
of property or de-contracted *cancel* cancelled out.

I Didn't, I Won't

I didn't start out to be difficult, but even
The cat gets jet lag and the first
Line was written in Cyrillic. Better than

The jet nag on my right (*Could you be more clear?*)
During an entire evening flight. She
Asked me "pussy's" name. 𝕭𝕚𝕥𝕥𝕪 𝕽𝖆𝖓𝖙, I said.

*What? It rhymes with "font" and "want"; or is it
"Rant" and "cant"? He's under my seat
Sound asleep on drugs. Won't you have some*

Too? Do you want those nuts? she asked,
Seeing them unopened on my tray beside
Three mini bottles of gin. *Win or lose,*

I said, *I don't start off to be difficult. Will you
Have one in Cyrillic? Have one, my dear,
In Old Church Slavonic? Will I have one what?*

*Or not, imperative. Or lines written for
The money that subscribed this mass.
Do we fast forever? I endeavor to please,*

So jeez, I won't be difficult! A sneeze.
Now just what did you mean by that? It was
The cat 𝕽𝖆𝖓𝖙 – *sleeping, but allergic to*

The feathers on your hat. Oh, that. I'll pull
Them out. *I think you doubt "I didn't"
And "I won't."* (*It's* even in the title.) *Here come*

Our dinners. Does that make us diners?
Dinars were devalued decades back.
They couldn't and they can't. Your axiom?

My axiom combines both do and don't.

Post-Anecdotal (with a New Third Part)

I

And then what? Then I thought of
What I first remembered:
Underneath some porch with Gide.
Oh, not with Gide. But after years & years
I read that he remembered what he first
Remembered, and it was that.

II

Not this: Someone calling me,
Johnny, Johnny. I was angry, hid.
It was humid, summer, evening.
I hid there sweating in the bushes
As the dark came down. I could
Smell the DDT they'd sprayed
That afternoon – it hung there in
The air. But so did the mosquitoes
That it hadn't killed. *Johnny!*
Oh, I'd not go back at all. I'd
Slammed the door on everyone.

III

Post antidotal: I sent for things when
I was sick I thought would make me well:
Tom Mix toys, pirate treasure maps,
Decoder rings. Better than the children
On my block, I liked my radio. (It told
You where to send the box tops and
The dime.) When I heard them outside

In the street with baseball bats & bikes,
I'd turn on the radio, and that would
Rub them out: erased by "The Shadow"
Like some parsed antic doodle.

Tourist Guide to Crete

Should you go to Crete
You must be discreet.
Between the roses
Among the briars
Autócthon the cat
Sees that the poses
Of human tourists
Make them the same
As the honest cits
Or municipal criers
And Orthodox wits
Who always are liars
In spite of their fame
As history's purists.
Take care when you speak.
And if you should meet
A cat at your feet
Tell him the truth.
He'll know that you lie
But only thereby
Can one greet in the street.
Be also discrete
(An *ete* for the beat)
Through a singular series,
And top of topology
Utterly open as set.
Your sure methodology's
Likely to fret
Through a fear of pathology.
Be discontinuous
Even in face of The Calculus.
Be feline as Aeschylus
(It's Autócthon's first name)
And efficacious

As any hypothálamus flame.
Count up to nine
And you'll do just fine.

A Hard Man Is Good to Find

Was the title of that
Famous story re *The Misfit*
That the editors insisted must be
Changed to the title
We all know and the book of
Fiction as we have it. But what
Made the serial killer serial
In his terrible desire was the
Old finding that he couldn't
Get it up.

I Copy That

says whiz kid joy stick guy, wiseass sticks
it to 'em, jerks a lever, pokes a button on his
droneboard, says my hashtag's all configured
out of deathknell, but I copy that okay okay —
an em of space, a dash of Hem or tough guy
lingo, that I copied on the ditto or the mimeo
in typewriter days when young to épater some
dumb bourgeois who asked *that what?* That
that I'd say, although I'd never get a reference
for another job I knew it with such rear guard
offense. Be proactive, then, nostalgic about all
the girls on all the summer swings for whom
you dittoed up your works with purple hands
in love with tactile letters you could feel with
fingertips while setting up the roller-spindle,
turning multiples of coded bomb blasts bleating
like a cocky goat to separate the sheep into
the tray for copies that proclaimed your need
to be a whiz at something but you weren't
yet sure at what that *that* that copied pointed
to much less when it might start to live and be.

Firing Neurons à la Valéry

To exhaust what's possible, there's a tax on
Zeno Elean — and how's it to be paid?
Even Pindar drops to his knees in the sun
Of *Midi le juste* . . . What's to be renewed?
Only the sea, not the graveyard at its edge,
Not the bodies rotting there, not the
Rate of exchange, or the short route to
The past. Cast Achilles in the leading role
And he freezes in his stride, struck by
An arrow never moving as it flies. Fall calls
The summer sun a tortoise shadow of
The soul. Mind's just a brain; even chance
Encounters beg a protein synthesis, long term
Potentiation, seascape reaching out from
Molecules to *agnosia* where abstract feeling
Is sensation that does not replicate or animate
Either cemetery or the sea. So sorry, breaker,
Dans un tumulte au silence pareil:
In tumult that's an equal of all silence.

Rodefer à la Villon

I always hoped I'd someday meet Mr. Rodefer.
Both of us from Ohio, but keen to leave the state.
Keen to leave the country, too. Rodefer came
from Bellaire, I come from Columbus. And we
were born in 1940, 1941. Bellaire's on the river,
the big Ohio, where the toll bridge figures in
a movie, *The Silence of the Lambs*. It's a town
of about 5,000. Columbus is the capital of the state.
It's always a relief if the person whose obit
you read is older, even if it's only a matter of months.
When I was in Columbus, I was bored. My guess
is that Rodefer was bored stiff in Bellaire.
Of course I can't be sure. Had we ever met, we
might have talked about these things. Did Villon
love Paris? In fact, I can imagine him in Columbus,
but not Bellaire, mainly because I've never been
there, though my mother was from Georgetown,
another small Ohio River town. Maybe we'd have
played Huck Finn and Tom together, but who
would have been who? Since I never met him,
I can't guess. There are places where the Ohio's
as majestic as the Mississippi, although never
as broad. Villon had a difficult life, and it may be
that Rodefer's versions of his poems get them
just about on the nose. Or, in the ear. Did he
go by Stephen or Steve? Had we ever met, I
would know, Ohio. The air was bad in Paris, but
Villon and Rodefer seem to have liked it anyway.
The B&O railway bridge in Bellaire also figured in
A film: *The Unstoppable*, bits of it shot on site.
Four Letters, a poem, also never seems to stop.
There were no poems in Columbus. Perhaps a
few in Bellaire. As for snow, we sometimes had
a lot of it. Shovel, shovel, shovel. In Columbus.
I'm not sure about Bellaire. But now I'll never meet
Mr. Rodefer. *Where are the snows of yesteryear?*

A Sinking Boat (2)

it's from a backwards *bateau ivre* said *i* and
doubtless what *they* would have said whenever
he as *one* walked off to Paris with it in his pocket
a rimbaud unknown uneducated all unwashed
and unsophisticated and uncouth a peasant as
for *me* I rowed his boat all via the Varèse version
new directions 1961 and starting on the Olentangy
or my local river as it was and where it flows
beside the football stadium and then within a bend
or two or three the state house where my father
was a *jedge* or *joustice* (*jurist*) categories morphed
if not the work itself by just a bit through all the
vowels a black *a* / a white *e* / a red *i* / a green *u* /
a blue *o* / and so then as *i* was red and that was
just the trouble and as *i* thought the rest were
yellow as in cowards with the jaundice oh your
own self or selfie portrait *jedge* / *joustice* / *jurist*
nor did any of them smell the slave ship's hold
pennants and flags! *they* flew them in the wake
of oil tankers making waves that spread their
filth on all the wings including mine a sad child
tried to float his boat in nearby little pond in
park full of sorrow it was farther off than *u* green
vowel but cold / cold with ice still at its edge
in even happy may of black *a* / white *e* / blue *o*
vowels out of order for the sake of rhyme / time
o trumpet call of miles at arthur's 502 club
1961 omega eyes lit up the whole spectrum yes
of casualties arising in the charity of sound! / child
from the shores of Olentangy wanting to be back
if blackness had produced a synesthesia unaccounted
for before / agnostic in the *a* of things and white
dust on *iou* for any invoice other than his own for
anti-grammar ambiguity chromatic in the pro
noun detective working nights in a defective town

ten people in that club and just the one red *i* or *me*
archepels sidéraus / e'd often seen 'em longing short
for europe's parapets & said e'd sail through beyond
the maelstroms hiding deep quiescent blue or green *u*
and all the gray hippocampus in hypotenuse had
struggled in a triangle of love not in august for augustus
but september for the ovid month my own birth and
deep honor to my other and my utter for ethereal
abstraction on the facebook wall just one line at a time
and one time at a line of white powder that he had never
tasted but was tested anyway a positive a charge that he
appealed as negative from both ends of his battery so
who could prove that he'd deranged the gas range already
let alone his senses in the sense that you might mean

III

After *Las Formas Puras*, after Lorca

i.m. Anthony Kerrigan

The pure shapes of things shake and are fall
ing under the cry of *bajo el cri cri*
and chirping of the six margaritas
daisies that I loved but now know deflower
when the men bent upon murdering me bend
down in cabinets and on cliffs and in cafés
where some flamenco guitarist breaks his fingers
on the grave accents \ \ \ breaks
his fingers on the acute

      / /

        hunting now
even in the graves under walls of tall iglesias
the well where *I am not* hides from
those who dug the gold from wisdom teeth
of the wise and dig it still and dig it
also from between my thin skeleton's bowed ribs
but *Ah*

      \ \

        will not find me any more but less
than six, the moon, *de pronto,* loss itself
disarticulated bones in hiding place   pues encore
my absence from *I am*
comprendo nonetheless the names
of pure shapes of things that shake and are fall
ing all loss los nombres under *cry cry*
the pure shaping things out of their somersault
out of themselves

After Quevedo

i.m. Octavio Paz

    not even lost in death the memory
of why we burned, and therefore still
a fire consuming all obsequious delay,
now polvo, dust, of a desire but still alive

    and aching, not even lost to you
within our common urn, urgent as an ash
still burning alma, soul, still
and moving toward you, la muerte, my amor –

    not even lost in death, memoria,
and feeling some reply, alma, memory and ash,
ash burning still, still
and moving toward you, dust & dust, ash

      alma and amor constant
      más allá de la muerte, constant

even in our common urn, polvo enamorado.

Icarus

ERIK LINDEGREN

His memories of the labyrinth go numb with sleep.
The single memory: how the calls and the confusion rose
until at last they swung him up from the earth.

And how all cleavings which have cried out always
for their bridges in his breast
slowly shut like eyelids,
and how the birds swept past like shuttles, like arrows,
and finally the last lark brushing his hand,
falling like song.

Then: the winds' labyrinth, with its blind bulls,
cacophonous lights and inclines,
with its dizzying breath which he through arduous
struggle learned how to parry,
until it rose again, his vision and his flight.

Now he is rising alone, in a sky without clouds,
in a space empty of birds in the din of the aircraft . . .
rising toward a clearer and clearer sun,
turning gradually cooler, turning cold,
and upward toward the spring of his blood, soul's cataract:
a prisoner in a whistling lift,
a seabubble's journey toward the looming magnetic air:
the bursting of the foetal membrane, transparently near,
and the vortex of signs, born of the springtide, raging of azure,
crumbling walls, and drunkenly the call from the other side:
Reality fallen
               without reality born!

(translated from the Swedish with Göran Printz-Påhlson)

The House of Headache

TOMAS TRANSTRÖMER

I woke up inside the headache. The headache is a room where I have to stay as I cannot afford to pay rent anywhere else. Every hair aches to the point of turning grey. There is an ache inside that Gordian knot, the brain, which wants to do so much in so many directions. The ache is also a halfmoon hanging down in the light blue sky; the color disappears from my face; my nose is pointing *downwards*; the entire divining-rod is turning down toward the subterranean current. I moved into a house built in the wrong place; there is a magnetic pole just under the bed, just under my pillow, and when the weather chops around above the bed I am charged. Time and again I try to imagine that a celestial bone-setter is pinching me through a miraculous grip on my cervical vertebrae, a grip that will put life right once and for all. But the house of headache is not ready to be written off just yet. First I have to live inside it for an hour, two hours, half a day. If at first I said it was a room, change that to a house. But the question now is this: Is it not an entire city? Traffic is unbearably slow. The breaking-news is out. And somewhere a telephone is ringing.

(translated from the Swedish with Lars-Håkan Svensson)

Two from *Des Petits Hommages*

Tomas Tranströmer

His Chinese friend had asked: *Do you hear
the tuba blast?*

0

He did, all along the coast
Or was it only in his head, drowning out the Mozart
welcoming the dead

&

Hashtag, as they say,
pressing fingers on their small machines
#stockholmarchipelago // stroke stroke

\#

Sapphics, said his friend,
touching with his finger TT's living lips
that could no longer speak
Too many Sapphics

RENÉ CHAR

As if encrypted as a code by the Maquis
"Julieta" "Cabassac"
were hiding in the truffles

just as René Char was hiding in the peasant cottage
in Provençe with potent radios
understood much later by a Yank to be what powered
Paradise Lost

radi / os

"a false proximity," thought Heidegger, but just the thing
to bring the news: *télégraphie sans fils*

#

A friend finds *notness* in all *sonnets*
while my student some years back, Yanbing Chen,
knocked at my window in the night

saying: "Done it! Done it!"
(for a translation seminar at Notre Dame,
the university
and not the great cathedral)

& pasted his new page against the glass:
Landscape Over Zero, by Bei Dao
it said
and Yanbing said

"Surprise! I've written it in Sapphics!"

A Backward *Zone*

after Guillaume Apollinaire

Slit
throat   sun
good
bye   good buy & least
last of Christ's obscure desires
fetish out of Oceania
walking home from Wherever
drinking whisky not His light
as night downdawns in justice
where the milkmen pick up bottles
from the street and otherwise
one is alone and humblemouth
from kissing cunt
of criminal new laughter's
child the old rite policeman on
the beat of warning woe
and everyone but you worn out

a two sous coffee with the wretches
standing at their ease   Wives in wigs
and chessmen stay at home
Wake up dawn down once more
on rue des Rosiers on rue des Ecouffes
the refugees who failed their exams
in Argentina shuffle now around
the Gare St. Lazare & smell like
floors in the broken down pissoirs
or rented rooms in criminal hotels
You'd been in Latin Cubicula
been in Leyden Amsterdam Marseilles
you'd taken ship and listened
to the Czech chansons sitting high

on watermelon piles
hands on the ghetto clock to pull
it backwards down
Happy journeys wasted youth
arrested taking paintings from the Louvre

That's you ok　　　　that's you
in *Les Soirées* December 1912
and thirty-three like poor
Villon　I'm working out of Anne Hyde Greet
myself but also Mr. Beckett whom
we all revere
although I'm sure you never met him
over drinks in your *Alcools* but
living forward in his Englished *Zone* and
backward in my own

Would you believe Our Lady blessed
me there in Chartres
my love is like a loathsome illness
driving a decline in liveliness
before those days when you'd have been
a monk & walk alone in human
traffic now the traffickers parading
with their women lash and leash
and fraternize with flyby pilots
vain as *les dauphins*
When you pray you pry a secret shame
and sham becomes you more than
all those Czech chansons you learned
abroad　Lyrebird & peacock
overcame the doves who wing it over
whingding hummingbirds from
human wars　　　　Ibis is the storked-out
bird from Africa but falcon will not
clutch your offered glove there's no
peace for great green dirigible

but field of Enoch and Elijah gadzooks
Apollinaire original as eye
of Jesus hovering above the aviation
and the *ave* not to speak of
gallows from which hang the amethyst
and pious child   You were
dressed in blue and white for incense
and for ceremonies of the redhead
with a torch your old friend
René Dalise ahead of you   Fine streets
the lives of greater men and sweet
stenographers with whodunits pocked
with winsome crime where all
the cars belong to Gertrude Stein

You've lived too long with Greece and Rome
so room enough to roam O now
O Eiffel Tower
So admit: At last you're weary
of this ancient world: *de ce monde ancien*

Camilla of the Volscians

from Aeneid, VII

I

                          . . . and also in the vanguard
came Camilla with her troop of horse,
terrifying in their bronze. This girl had never
been a weaver, not at any loom, or even one
Minerva favored in her youth. This girl
was a warrior, one who sped like crazy wind
when riding over unripe grain, fed all winter
on the grapes of autumn's wrath. This season
saw her ride with Agamemnon's son, and so with
Virbius, sent there by Aricia; ride with Umbro,
master of the snakes – rune-singer, herb-plucker –
binder of wounds and scar-tender of the Latins.
Aeneas saw her, gliding over the fields, one
who might have come in spring anger riding from
the very waves. Men stood in wonder, gazing
as she rode, awe and fear become for them
a measure of the hero's robe she wore, blowing
in the wind, cinched at her neck with the brooch
that once had bound her hair, now flowing golden
and uncombed.
                          She raised her steel-pointed staff
in her right hand, led, in the bright dawn sun,
her goaded, glowing cavalry . . .

II
Camilla, blood-sister fore-type of the Roman-slaying
Boadicea, enters Virgil's Latin hand Englished
by the generations – Douglas, Surrey, Ralegh,
Dryden, and the rest . . .
                                   she glows

in language, glows *as* language, bronzed and ready

for her book, heard by all of them as death-dealer in her
death-throes all the way to the American Fitzgerald,
finished with his *Iliad,* done with his *Odyssey,* reading from
a manuscript, not yet published, to a few of us, friends
of his friend Sandeen, at Notre Dame, and well before the
excerpts in *Conjunctions, Kenyon, Poetry,*
circa 1981–1983 –

"For Penny," read the dedication. Penelope, who else?

That was in another age. And when I taught my seminar
a student even in those days complained: "What does Virgil
have to do with our topic, 'The Generation of Robert Lowell?'"
And I said: "Think about it," but I don't know that he did.

Camilla, then . . .
                    Camilla in original Latinity:
leading her horsemen, bright in her bronze.
Turnus less than her as hero, less than her in arms.
Defender of the indigenous, with no confused desires,
not a jealous lover or a would-be king.

Lost in the wind is someone's "No more fighting.
Not for you, Turnus. Why not have some pity for
your people? Why engulf the Latins in their blood
like a numbskull Mussolini. Cool your testicles
in River Tiber; calm your lust and jealousy.
Otherwise, you'll see your warrior girl killed for
the other one you only want to fuck. Would you
sacrifice a Latin Joan of Arc for marriage? Tell her
to retreat, tell her not to spill her Volscian blood
for just the likes of you . . ."

Then right in his path:

                    she and her entire cavalry
dismount. They stand there in their hundreds

and she says: "I will go and fight Aeneas' horsemen; you
can guard the city gate. It's nothing much, but
you can do a little. As for me, Diana will protect me
if some greater god does not oppose her love.

Grotesques from the Anglo-tabloids yet to come:
"Diana" and "Camilla" quarrel over Charles. But who
would want him? Who would want Lord Turnus?
How many lines did Virgil skip? Sitting in his Princeton
digs, the German Hermann Broch tries to do the math,
to scan the lines, and think of what he'll talk about
at dinner with the table full of physicists.
How did all of them end up
together in New Jersey? Most of them are thinking all
about the works of Oppenheimer, Fermi, Bohr.
Broch's thinking all about his Roman poem. The others
think about the bomb, the quanta in the quantum
physics. Who cares if a poet wanted to destroy his poem?
Augustus cared, he thinks. Perhaps the dialogue between
the two of them could make a book. Does anybody want
more war? Maybe that could be a theme. Women in
the cavalry, women tank commanders, women spies.
What choice would Camilla make? The bronze-armored virgin
and Diana's darling girl.

      When I came to poetry, it was
in anthologies edited by Untermeyer and Oscar Williams.
Both of them anthologized themselves, and Untermeyer
anthologized his wife as well. I was maybe sixteen, seventeen
and had no understanding of the log-rolling in those times.
But Jean Starr Untermeyer Englished Herman Broch,
a gift her husband maybe never understood. For decades
The Death of Virgil was a title out there over the horizon
with *Ulysses*, *Doctor Faustus*, and *The Waves*. And then at some point,
Virgil spoke: *Kill the book. What is a mere book*
if beauty cannot tell the truth?
      Augustus came to claim it.

Or at least that makes a story now. Then the poet said
"My Emperor," or maybe even "Ah, my friend Octavian."
Augustus came for him in Athens, but he knew the poet
courted death, the poem his own immortal life. Even though
it wasn't finished, even though the poet wished it burned.
"Where is it?" asked the greatest man alive. "Right there in
the trunk on which you see my slave-boy sitting, silent.
Why not read again the words I wrote upon the shield
while I try to finish, even if it's only in my mind . . ."

Finish with some kind of unfinished business? That would
be the thing. The shield told too much, and he'd erase it
if he could. But that's the bit Octavian liked best, and there
he sat, Augustus. There sat Broch at dinner with the fathers
of the atom bomb. What was a mere slaughter of these
native Latins? A few spears thrown, some arrows in the eye
or throat or genitals; some heads lopped off. A pity that
the poet had already loosed Juturna all disguised as Camers,
and inspired the augur, Toluminius, to interpret Jove's
golden bird as taloned omen. "Bomb them till they shit their
pants," he screamed. "Bomb them till they sit like Job in
dust and blood and vomit all irradiated by the stormcloud.
Kill especially Menotes, war-hater, peace-lover, hugger
of trees and fisherman in Lerna rivers where his worthless
father merely cultivates some peasant plot of land."
Juno said: "No truce! Start the fighting up again because you
lost Camilla and the only sister's recourse is revenge."
And so Juturna spreads the rumor and the poet sickens in
his own unrevisable revision. He'd tried to do it once, but now
he could no longer even trace his plot. Camilla or Juturna?
Which girl was which? The Emperor would know . . .
or wouldn't know . . .
                    And sat there smiling.
Broch looked up and asked: "Are there women physicists?
Did anybody say they'd marry you if you did this work
for Harry Truman?" Someone said, "We worked for Roosevelt."
And Broch: "Virgil worked for Caesar, but Juturna was the sister

of the Latin hero; Camilla was commander of his allies; Lavinia was the contested bride." "And who's Penny," asked a Princeton Fellow, thumbing decades later in a paperback. This was in the Eighties. "I suppose she was the poet's wife."

The Major Odes

The notes that tell us chopping off the ear
really meant decapitation yield a click away
the flicks on television clearly showing how
the head-choppers of ISIS chop off heads, not ears,
and one can hear the screaming terror even when
the video is shrouded in a wholly silent dread.
Skype, sometimes, brings beheadings to us one or two
removes, all commercials by conglomerates
advertising Mao Zedong brand soups and yes
suppositories.
              The Greater Odes are
"poems containing history," although like us they
fail utterly in their containment. History rolls over them
and over those old poets and their poems; it buries us
beside them with our own. "History Will Bury You."
Remember? Comrade K in the UN and Mr. Maximus in
Saint Elizabethan pilgrimage, complaining as the figure
of young Mencius, pupil of the Master, bitches about
"Coolie Verse" and Ezra's "vertu/you do" rhyming in a
crabbed hand when Mao has morphed into a
short selling hedge fund. Though I don't know a whorehouse
from a palace, I can quote the timetable well enough for
local trains and lay down rails –
              1960 Second Printing
by Grove Press. Maximus was still in Jargon/Corinth that same year
and me with *Shih-ching* in hand, copyrighted by the President
and Fellows of the Harvard College. At eighteen, I thought that
gave the thing a bit of clout in spite of Mr. Mencius or Maximus
and look at this: an introduction by Achilles Fang, a real name
celebrated by all endodontists everywhere. Acetaminophen
only for a root canal these days. The good painkillers
now ground up with heroin and sold to addicts on the street,
vide William Burroughs, well ahead of the suburban matrons
now doped up as he was but without a muse. Charlie Parker,

Miles Davis – who'd have guessed at Birdland that the best
thing on the street would one day be prescriptions written
by some arthritic white lady's doc –

resulting, no way, in opium's war, but just a wink
and nod and just say no. Meanwhile major odes still sing
the emperors, doing it or not, addicted to the power.
Power, say, of Wen – the diligent, the source of many
generations bringing to a birth the knights of Zhou
and a succession thanks to Jiang Yuan. Do we all of us
emerge from melon seeds? A gourd appears, says
Arthur Waley, like an ark. Does Mencius dispute this?
Maximus himself read no Chinese. And yet, as pupil of
the master, he complained. But King Wen harried
his life. Harried Arthur Waley, harried Ezra Pound.
Saint Elizabeths was an asylum for the criminally insane.
Was King Wen a criminal? Was Kung? That Muso and
John Adams were Confucians, Old Son had his doubts.
Yet, as Mencius, continued visits alternating with
Miss Bishop's. I wonder if they met. Could they have learned
anything from contradictions in each other's style?
I mean right there, in the middle of an Ode, in some hallway
of the institution now rebuilt as NSA's electronic studio.
What musics of an unimagined kind
darting now from Major Odes on odd fellow frequency?
Who kept insolence at bay? "There were those," says an Ode,
but were they "zealous in their task"? Who climbed
the foothills of Mount Han? Let me guess that it wasn't
Chiang Kai-shek. Great Dignity demanded Lady Jiang of Zhou.
Major odes of the period, smart money and big features
offer blind trust and double bind by military futures built
up out of ears all clipt and fallen, heads of enemies but also
doubtless onetime friends: Kuomintang sang *auld lang syne*.

Wen was wan at some point way back then, wandered with
no dignity into a dingy time. A hallway dark and narrow
full of nitwits, noncoms, and a man in a newspaper

hat with a bat in his brain – Wu, "The Martial," and his brother
Duke of Zhau, and Cheng – my former student Mr. Feng
telling me in seminar just who they were and then
politely also saying, *you do know of course that Mr. Pound's
and Mr. Fenollosa's understanding of the Chinese Written
Character was too characteristically well off the mark . . .
although I do agree that without character no one can play
a right music for the Odes –*

                    so don't confuse, he said,
*the mythman Barleycorn, Lord Millet, with historical
King Wen,* and when my in-law, Wayland Young, Lord Kennet,
visited the prisoner in his cell, his host was not assailed
by the demons of remorse, but only nervous ticks, reading
poems in progress to the guest, and new translations,
letters from old friends and lawyer briefs and medical reports,
looking up to say: *Your accent tells me you're a Brit
but how come, Lord of the Kennet, you're called Wei Lan Yung?
My wife's a Brit,* he said, *a Shakespeare in fact, but known
in this our Capital as Ezra Pound's "Committee," the authority that
saves old Kung, master of the pupil Mencius, from hanging
on the yard arm of the Ship of State . . .*

                           The Greater Odes
tell us that the state shifts its boundaries, seeds its fields,
trains its young, honors its traditions. Godwit flies – such a
bird in Western Zhou? – where Nitwit once had sung.
Along the Yellow River to the Yellow Sea, one was treading
on the footprint of the maker, one was birthing from
the egg of a dark bird, one gave agriculture to his people,
one married Lady Jiang and sired sons: Bei Yong, Wei
Zheng, Qui, Tang, Qin, Chen – these were states of land and
mind celebrated in the airs. Among heirs, one was called "the civil"
and another "Earl of the West": One married Lady Xin, begat
Wu Wang, "the Martial," whose brother was the regent
for King Cheng . . . And it goes on in spite of the disputed
texts and terrible translations . . . Heaven drew them with
its whistle made of clay, its bamboo flute, listing things
upon its tally, wayward people, wanting. Even when

the grains were lucky, grass thick, millet black, and divination
by the tortoise accurate, they sometimes
failed even where the sow thistle made the fields sweet
and drummers did not tire and Wen's tower was rebuilt
for grand initiations where, in spite of that, in spite of fit
propitiations, people of the Middle Kingdom grew exhausted
even with the royal clans for rafters, clan heirs as fortress,
those especially in a time of drought who stood above
the grave of Mu shaking in their bones because they had been
chosen to be tomb-mates who could not be ransomed by
their kin or otherwise avoid what the short straw and
wilting patch of celery had done to them: Made their honor
out of death's companionship

    though Kung of London/Pisa/Saint Elizabeths
"said nothing of the life after death"
but only said again and yet again

                        study the *Shi-ching*
in the old days the poets would leave blanks
for "known unknowns" / for "unknown unknowns"
gaps were filled in later
by the hunters lifting up and looking under stones
even in the ballads of our own

IV

Three Act Play

Mr. G approaches Mr. B. The latter is sitting on a rock. An empty bench beside him.

Act I

Mr. G: I don't suppose you've been sitting here long. Mr. B: I have, as a matter of fact. Since about 1853. Mr. G: Mind if I join you? Mr. B: Happy to have some company. Mr. G: You're not waiting for someone? Mr. B: Oh, no! Mr. G: That's a relief, I can tell you. Mr. B: A relief? Mr. G: Well, yes! Mr. B: No one ever had to wait for me. I was always there. That was the beauty of it. Mr. G: Me, I never showed up. That was the duty of it; the gravity; the depravity. Mr. B: We should introduce ourselves, don't you think? Mr. G: I think not. Anonymity is best. Mr. B: Is best? Mr. G: Is best of all, unless? Mr. B: Unless what? Mr. G: Unless we were the last of the lost. Mr. B: The least of the last? Mr. G: Unless we used first names. Mr. B: Christian names! Mr. G: And yours is? Mr. B: Bart. Mr. G: Bart? Mr. B: Bart. Mr. G: I'm Gobsmack, myself. Mr. B: Christian? Mr. G: Only in a missionary sense. Mr. B: Missionary position? Mr. G: Missionary possession. Mr. B: When you're on top. Mr. G: I was never on top. Mr. B: You bided your time. Mr. G: I was sublime. Mr. B: In those days? Mr. G: On all the bidets. Mr. B: Perhaps I was your rhyme. Or your mime. Mr. G: On all the bidets of the world. Mr. B: You were sublime. Mr. G: In those ways. Mr. B: In all the clichés. Mr. G: I was never on time. Mr. B: But you were positionary, possessionary. Mr. G: Sedentary! Mr. B: And yet more stationery than stationary. Mr. G: You've not read my guy's sad book.

Mr. G suddenly sits down on the bench beside Mr. B's rock. Mr. B gives him a surprised look, then reaches over and takes his hand. They hold hands throughout Act II.

Act II

Mr. B: But you've had a look at mine. Mr. G: It's why I stopped by. Mr. B: Sat down. Mr. G: Stood up. Mr. B: You liked it? Mr. G: Gobsmacked by it, in fact. Mr. B: Gobsmacked is it? Mr. G: It was. Mr. B: Do you know my guy? Mr. G: Your guy? Mr. B: You don't mean my boss? Mr. G: I mean your guy. Mr. B: Well, yes, my guy. Mr. G: Was he gay? Mr. B: Some people say. And yours? Mr. G: He was one for the ladies. Mr. B: For the laddies? Mr. G: The ladies. Mr. B: Have it your way. Mr. G: The way you prefer. Mr. B: *Mais je ne préfère pas.* Mr. G: Not to? Mr. B: You've got it. Mr. G: I get it? Mr. B: You've got it or you've thought it. Mr. G: Pah! Mr. B: *Pas de ça.* Mr. G: You think? Mr. B: I think so. Mr. G: At any rate, you often preferred . . . Mr. B: Not to. Mr. G: Not to . . . what? Mr. B: Just not to. Mr. G: *J'aimerais mieux pas.* Mr. B: A way of putting it. Mr. G: A translation? Mr B: A Preference. Mr. G: Work! Mr. B: That was my guy. Mr. G: Your guy? You mean your boss. Mr. B: Oh, no. He was someone else. Mr. G: You didn't like your job. Mr. B: I lost the job. Mr. G: But when you had it, did you like it? Mr. B: There were things I couldn't do. Mr. G: Couldn't or wouldn't. Mr. B: Couldn't and wouldn't. Mr. G: At the request of your boss? Mr. B: He was at a loss, sometimes, for words. Mr. G: But you were always there. Mr. B: I was always there. Mr. G: When he came in? Mr. B: And when he went out. Mr. G: He was gobsmacked, I take it. Mr. B: Take it or leave it. Mr. G: You were there all the time. Mr. B: I was there overtime. Mr. G: Were you paid over time? Mr. B: I was paid to begin. Mr. G: But not paid to end. Mr. B: I was not paid to end. Mr. G: With what did you begin? Mr. B: I began with a pen. Mr. G: To copy, perhaps? Mr. B: To copy, my ass! Mr. G: And all of it legal? Mr. B: A bit of a giggle. Mr. G: A kind of black mass. Mr. B: I copied my ass. Mr. G: How many came to attend? Mr. B: There were about ten.

Mr. G drops Mr. B's hand and very suddenly stands up.

Act III

Mr. G: As for me, I always delayed. Mr. B: You delayed. Mr. G: I delayed. Mr. B: Delayed doing what? Mr. G: Anything at all. Mr. B: But nonetheless they waited? Mr. G: Maybe for you? Mr. B: Hardly for me! Mr. G: For you. Mr. B: How many for me? Mr. G: Just three. Mr. B: That's for the rhyme. Mr. G: Thanks for your time. Mr. B: How many for you? Mr. G: Just two. Mr. B: And your guy? Mr. G: My guy. Mr. B: Your guy. Mr. G: He was convinced that I never showed up. Mr. B: My guy was gay. Mr. G: My guy was one for the girls, but he was convinced that I never showed up. Mr. B: As for me, I never left. Mr. G: I delayed. Mr. B: But it played pretty well in those days. Mr. G: Those days! Mr. B: Those ways. Mr. G: And a light shining out in the bay. Mr. B: Were you ever at home? Mr.

G: I was always alone. Mr. B: Alone! Mr. G: Never at home! Mr. B: I felt cold as any stone. Mr. G: I was right as rain! Mr. B: Hedonistic! Mr. G: Sadistic! Mr. B: End of the page coming up. Mr. G: End of an age. Look out! Mr. B: I'm looking. Mr. G: Out! Mr. B: At what? Mr. G: At what becomes of us. Mr. B: Nothing becomes of us. Mr. G: Nothing? Mr. B: Nothing less. Mr. G: Nothing more? Mr. B: Nothing more.

Mr. B and Mr. G both produce large placards, which have been lying face down under the bench. They turn them face forward, toward the audience:

Mr. B's Placard: NOTHING LESS?
Mr. G's Placard: NOTHING MORE.

Postcolonial Chicken

1. Texts

"When he brought the chicken into the hotel lobby he became embarrassed, so he stuffed it inside his double-breasted serge and went up in the lift smelling of spit-roast."
— Salman Rushdie, *The Satanic Verses*

"I had been given a roasted chicken . . . but I had no knife. I ate it over the wastepaper basket, aware as I did so of the smell . . . I was ending my day like a peasant, like a man reverting to his origins, eating secretively in a dark room."
— V.S. Naipaul, *The Enigma of Arrival*

2. Enigmas

Of Departure: *Chicken à la King*
Of Arrival: *Chicken Cacciatore*
Of Return: *Chicken Tandoori*

But why did the chicken leave its roost? How did the chicken lay a golden egg? What were the chicken bones doing in the trash? Who, after all, had caught the chicken on the run? And who, but, but, confound it, found the egg?

Duck, duck, duck, duck, goose: 'twas Goose who laid the golden egg. Duck and Chicken took it on their frigate out to sea, became themselves thereafter fowlmix takeout fricassee. Cacciatore spoke in *à la King* to Giorgio escaping a conscription with some loose change beneath *Nostalgia for the Infinite* on unframed canvas in a red caboose. In his painting on the hotel wall, but, but, de C's great egg casts forth a shadow on the two young men, Mister A and Mister B. The egg is very large and the men are very small. They gesture at each other, but they do not speak. Paintings do not speak. They look like this or look like that. Speakers speak, but not like A and B. The egg continues casting shadow when the men walk out beyond the frame and then along the wall and out the door. Gone beyond their calling, their gestures still remain. They were peckish. And so they waved their arms like wings and flew. A little bit. The clue of it, a clew. [1. *Greek Mythology*: The ball of thread used by Theseus to find his way out of the labyrinth. But also necessary if you want to fix your sail as you come about. But A and B: They haven't got a clew.]

3. Chicken à la King

In the little room were no silver-bright and monogrammed utensils. The dresser drawer contained no Yoruba Ibejis or a small statue of Ganesh. No peaceful Buddha sat, legs crossed, upon a comfy pillow on the bed. But there was, but, but, a book. Not Confucian *Analects* and not the *Tao Te Ching* and no *Qur'an* (spelled in those days with a K, *Koran*) but something left by Gideons. (What tribe, but, or nation they?) Forbidden menu was a centerfold of duties from their *Deuteronomy. Now they're on to me,* thought A, *but not,* thought B, *the dude that oughta be:* Decline, it said, the meat

of every beast that cheweth cud and is of cloven hoof or those of cloven hoof yet cheweth not the cud nor them that yet divide the cloven hoof as camel hare and coney for they chew the cud but don't divide the hoof or swine because they do, but, but, divide the hoof yet cheweth not the cud. No mention of the bird that clucks and pecks but does not often fly. Inside the Georgio great egg there was another room like this one in another egg and inside that another all with but a room like that and but inside of that another room like this and so on, but, but =

each containing Mr. A and Mr. B until they exit from the frame and walk along the wall and finally speak in *Chicken à la King:*

Mr. A: *My real name is Shadow*
Mr. B: *My real name is Shire*

They put a seal on that until they saw that someone scoffed. An anthropologist. Not to be accused of it by Mr. A whose name, but, but, is Shadow now. Not to be amused by Shire, formerly the very self of Mr. B. Their share in this but crumbs fallen from some high table (Trinity or King's?) golden in the egg. Would you rather nibble fatwa or retain your noble pride? When they were very young, therefore, they listened on a radio at teatime to a program called *The Shadow Knows.* The knowledge let the language of the home fire burn. It wasn't, but, but, entirely anthropologist, however and, that moment when they stood beside *Enigma of Arrival*, departing soon enough on its begin again.

Before the butbut and therefore, the knot of all distinctions and degrees, a cause célèbre and all about decrees (as if inside of *He decreed it* but it anyway was not not so). Shire and Shadow had a shipping spirit there to make enigma of arrival anagram itself imagine, as it does, almost, when just a little i is added on. But drumstick doesn't serve as Georgio's requirement for *spécialité de la maison*, although the latter coughs up an anyway as wishbone in the golden egg. Other bones are, chuck it, in the basket with the claim check of gadsblood and cloven hooves goddamnit and the cuds of animals escaped from *Deuteronomy*, Gideons in swift, but, although, pursuit.

4. Chicken Cacciatore

It was winter out. The snow fell. Influenza stalked the native population. Shire and Shadow stayed indoors, stuffing coins in shilling heaters, practicing a cultivated conversation. You're a square said Mr. Shadow. You're all round said Mr. Shire. You're a squandered opportunity. You're a ransomed renegade. You're my Cromwell. You're my Cavalier. Neither of us dear, is *haute cuisine*, however much we may aspire to caviar. Try their roast beef and Yorkshire pudding, pal. Their soggy peas. Fish and chips with vinegar, all wrapped in Tabloid. Local girls were *chicks* before they gentrified as Sixties and generic *birds*. Cacciatore, but, but, means *hunter* to the enigmatic women and the egocentric chefs.

5. Chicken Tandoori

Oh well, Tandoori. Treat with cayenne and turmeric and chili powder till it's red as mad dog the Englishman out in the noonday sun. Kundan Gujral and mate Jagiji ran a kitchen in a Peshawar deli called De Chirico's. Although this was well before partition, the times included clock and egg and someone running with a, but, but, a hoop and stick. It took the world by storm. By *strum und drang*. In such weather one does not set sail. They say that certain London ethnics serve up in their restaurants horsemeat and alley cats, but who would know the difference as the wing and drumstick are so goodly red (though very badly read). Shire and

Shadow once again depart their room and step out the canvas in the egg into the street. A strike is on promoting *Hiraeth* on the outside. Inside now is anybody's guess. In the Welsh? In the sherbit, chicken heads mixed in the cheese. Jeez, mahn, I'll take fuck-all of that. Oh, why not share a bit with friends? But no trumpets for tandoori, but, but, except as crumpets for the Enigmatics (cult that agents of the anyway are infiltrating even now). And no longing for Colonial before the Post, who consecrates the host. What you want is in the mail or the mall. Arrival and departure and return are all peck and flap without a tangible: Meet them in the tangos dancing on a tangent plane contingent as a tantamount of Tottenham Court Road.

The M's's

I

. . . and the lot falls, and he's
among them. A strange company he keeps,
to whom he must surrender now. He's
on an island at the door. And she – for M is also
female – she is near a beach, waiting for her
lover on the grassy side of an Atlantic dune.
And they are all of me I am of them.

The bicycle he pedals with his little case
of watches. What time is it? He'll sell you, a *voyeur,*
the brand *voyageur*. But does that mean he's strung
to theory in those cogs and things? With strings
attached, he took the care to let his face become
all peaceful once again. For he was selling time
to coincide with rhyme in uncounted moments there
between two pillars carved of solid night with
darker night between, privileged points from
which observers see each other clearly and at once.
Which hardly meant he'd killed the lonely girl.
He was only there, reciprocal. She was only waiting for
her Ms, as M, upon the grassy side of the dune.
Lot fails in the Ethiopian and Vulgate if you
should say *look!* a Kalphi for the goat and not the sheep
appears in which the stones are placed and one
says *Game,* the other *Gallows*, and it's oh geez it's Judas
and I swear I didn't do it, officer, it's girls on grass
and don't you know it's legal now? No one any longer
studies bimbo Mss.
                    Banjo on his knee:
Can see the scenery uncertainly to say, and out of date,
forgotten. Does he take the name in vein?
Or open up the latter with a new orthography?

Men have said that M might like those friends
who pulled a tongue stiffened by the truth
in an estate precarious in pride lang syne & longer
life: M would not have hurt a one. Not anyone.
A one or a two and three; a four or five may be
in *that* book anyway. In another he might smother
her. He'd forgotten too his Kingdom. Crazy salad
in the Second Great Awakening. Drowsy in a clutch
of Mss and reaching for her breast, he'd beat that
story with his best. An onion, please. I like it with
the sliced tomatoes on the side. Vinegar and oil.
Blood and Soil, you Fascist prick!
Oil on water. I don't really care, just so you make it
look like him and not like someone else.

                                      Last we hear
in first Ms at 1/26 is just before the speaking
out in cloven tongues of fire and his departure out
of text to sit for his portrait with the pope.
I mean the one by Masolino, 1428, with Gregory the Great.
His emblem is an axe and with it does he figure forth
the murder in the Ms R-G, or is he just a woodsman?
Hangs in London now. But up near the dyke where
waters from baptismal wells are held to mix
with barks and pulp in papers for his books he has
his work. She takes his penis in her hand & says *expel*
and he says *marry me* and then they say together
Oh but we're espoused to others so one might
just anyway *excel* at binding up the second book or third.
The fourth and fifth; the sixth and seventh books:
They're in the lost domain, so if you wish to see, they
have to hear you, C? E.A.R. has versed him blank
and vested him in black. T.R.'s poet was a time-checker
in the New York subway until R got him M's old
despised position in the customs house. But there were
no dykes in going up or down – only lusty
heteros, running rapidly on waves into a narrow gorge
a litter bottle in anticipation of their broken necks.

He could not swim. But she had come
to dine with him
                         . . . & waits at hundred halfcrown dune
as altar and as hostess both. She'd sallied forth
To hide among the words that drop beside the butterflies
that hover blue among the flowers in enormous numbers now
that it's begun and finished both, and she is walking with
him back from what they've done to asphalt parking lot
(a far cry from larking among saints, 1/26)
her bare feet covered with the sand to give
their tryst away in shaken sheets at home where trust
can only rhyme with lust do not say dust.
And she had said *do with me what you want* and he
had put her in an alphabet they'd both draw upon in speech
unlike the dawn they sought to celebrate
and more like night . . .
                         . . . light of liminal perception
fails her, but falls. Because he brought it sans a
corkscrew, cracked the neck of the merlot upon a rock,
and cut their lips on it, the wine and blood together
ran down their naked bodies as libation to the hour.
No presidents have favorite starving poets
any longer, though I think Mr. Bill once gifted Monica
with *Leaves of Grass*. T.R. often read three books a day
and valued mastery in motion. However, ass our hero chased
among the dunes belonged to another as in Ms R-G where
he himself is seized with panic, fills in blanks by
multiplying numbers in his head, fumbles in his pocket & then
hoists a gold-plated watch: *I'm selling time. It's time*
for crime and punishment, you think? Your mouth is covered
not with blood and wine, but ink.
Why no words in *Acts* that reference what he did?
He didn't do? A thing? The Mss take wing, and multiply. His
press agent got him painted with the Pope. Popped her cherry
did he, cut her throat? Depends on whether
she was sheep or goat.
Depends on whether he was dupe or just a dope. And then
it's there outside the picture, quote unquote.

II

Oy Vey, Mr. Precedent, OK, but why not make it evident –
the outside of the inside then, the lemon tree beyond
the limning marginal gloss, the monk's menacing gargoyle
on the top of capital column reproduced initial letter
from his copywork? As we among this order value well
just that kind of wrong over any copyright, begin again
as in *the girl's body was discovered in the morning*
at low tide. Tide low at morning in discovered was a
body girl's. He heard the news while he was drinking an
aperitif at the café *the at aperitif an drinking was he*
while news the heard he all because they herded sheep
and goats where popit agents Poped and multiplied
the picture into referential acts. Reverential acts, that is
or isn't: So we may continue. And I said the council counsels
fear for every year or so an M with Ms appears at closing time
inclining toward an acquisition that is unsustainable,
third cupboard standing in the fourth corner with
the fifth or sixth chairs unsteady on their broken legs.
Legs broken their on unsteady chairs sixth and fifth
the with a corner fourth the near standing cupboard
third, look out! The neck of the merlot bottle's broken
so is her's. And may it please the court. *Me, a law unto*
myself I said you know that M's father was a judge who
juggled as he wriggled on the bench. Grandfather too.
Singsally says that everybody's Family Bible's full of babble
bullshitting tales of other times and awesome acts, rhymes
far better at the bellfitting nightlight in the hall you creep
on down on all fours your fives a handspan and a
minor third on the piano. Or play it with your elbows
as the Monk would sometimes do his tonsure hidden
under some weird hat and not the hood of cowl. After
elbows he would stand and twist and turn all dervishy
was he autistic or was all of this just nuts and bolts
of his technique? Ms. R-G also does it elbows and as
many repetitions as required. These are verbatim

sometimes and it throws things off. These are
verbatim sometimes and it throws things off if time
and place are counted or accountable. In newspaper
lingo *leader's* a forgotten term in journalism school
where everything's TV and not a great man or woman
in a photograph appearing in a column with a gargoyle
on top when I myself against the rules took a snap
of M in London at the great art museum beside the
pope (Gregory) who said I'm Gregory and M I'm glad to
meet you and so shake (they did) their hands, a *lieder*.
Then they both took off their shoes and shook the sand
out of their socks alarmed that it might give away an
assignation in the dunes. But she was dead by now
with broken neck beside the one about an archivist
another in blank verse a telling way to tell a toll at once
bells bells bells bells bells
the patronage gone missing from the pocket of
your pants. He pulled hers down. But that was all he
did besides the rest excluded by consensus in his
Ms and Mss and M's's MMs

                                all damned for obfuscation
you my dear transparent singularity
whole person, female as Ms. Steiner said not Stein who had it
in and on and in and on and this and this and that
and then and then and now until she ran out of breath.
'Tis death to run out of breath, though Mss in plural
grants a longer life and M's's and MMs so go
configure out beyond the *on,* it all takes off and flies
which is a true comfort, comforter, since daughter's dowry
was never paid. And why is that? The why of it involving
field of corn with evangelicals she hung with who,
flashlights in their hands, awaited Prophet marching
toward them with a burning torch. A son of M
who spoke in English (why not Hebrew, Latin, Greek?)
and told her how her parents were the Devil's own
and she a daughter not of man but, God help us, God alone.
It was something else I tell you when she lay down cruciform

beside the table in our living room and shouted out *O God
I beg you get the Devil from this house Amen!* Sing Goddamn
as Grandfather used to say, stuck on an opinion for the court
or patriotic speech. Poor father of neutrino also zapped by
dream-daughter/mother/wife as Chinese sage whose observations
disapproved of CPT and Parity by way of the weak force
(but strong stress) 0.00000000000001 (which is VERY weak)
and so concedes that God is a lefthander after all,
and maybe gay. Would you trade your
DNA for mine? *Nein.* Oy Vey, as we began, and Prophet enters
history as ugly, I can tell you, as it gets. Someone else's
daughter fell for him in 1832 in Sing Sing, righteous man
he claimed, and sparked by Sherpa shapeshifter operating
out of plants and animals, an *animula* now, who, grown
all menacing on meth and Free Masonry, would teach
and temporize as patriotic semen streamed in the firmament.
Levite priesthood would replace the markets in America,
amen. The mystic Hen would lay a Gnostic egg.
M's lover then, although a Hudson Valley slave by God
by birth, was semi-literate and therefore when she
stumbled through a passage in a book about the Jesus Christ
aborted by the *look back to Egypt* crowd imagined him
a venerable man like others she had learned about from M
like Lafayette, George Washington. Beside the rustic fireplace
John of Leyden in his spirit-form had left, aligned with scissors
meant at the right astral moment to remove all facial hair,
the axe from Masolino, 1428. She sallied out as Sally, brazen
girl who'd do a full frontal selfie of her full frontal self.
How many manikins at last inspired the bare Brazilian cunt?
Not M's. She was, although a lusty kind of broad, well behind
the curve living in a novel published circa 1976. Please note
the date of that. I lived that year in Cambridge and I well
remember the centennial. 200 years. A young country still,
but post-colonial. And post-post-colonial, you crook.
Popularity is for the plebs, said M, looking for his image in

III

another book
                    where Sally Me hears Jerry say
so let us marry! although perhaps I'm really not
your type, or you're not mine. You always were inclined
to grope the girls with bigger breasts, although I tried
to turn you on to make a wish upon . . .
ridiculous! To make you fawn, in fact, on meley me & turn
your back on your old life, your wife. The marriage plot is always
full of strife, my dear. Where could we live? Only in
a book, read beneath a green light on a pier that flashed out
Fuck Me Please. But oh don't give me any dread disease.
Focused on the Massolino M, still emitting spectral colors
all laid down six hundred years ago. I forgot the corkscrew
so you simply broke the neck of the merlot and after
that broke mine, but in a different book. Look, I loved you
Jerry but I coveted a covenant where only necrophiliacs
can neck and fondle, though I don't admit complicity
in murder. Mother always told me that contestants ought
to cry out *Christ me*, as in *King Me* in a game of checkers.
Neckers in the adolescents' cars haven't got a thing on us.
Abolition in its day had nothing over Prohibition.
It's all in the shun of things, the dings and dongs. I suck
on one I really like until the rights turn into wrongs.
Regress to redress of grievance. It's a law. My tight jeans,
my meager means. You said we shouldn't be reckless.
Too many others involved: My husband, your wife, the kids.
Why doesn't the sun stand still? Reversing, we revert now
to the lot. Lot number 30744299. The house there only
let to live in. You and me. Live-in, love it, neighbor.
M's of course my married name. And he's nothing but
an em of space between two words, like –
like that – like that. In our day everyone still smoked,
especially intellectuals. Less so the homosexuals, you know?
Ahead, as one now says, of the curve. Nervous Nellies
Lyndon Johnson called us in those days. Why did you have

children, Jerry? Why did I? It's all American as apple pie,
my dear. But you can smell my fear. I wouldn't hear a
damn thing that you said at first. Trying to seduce me.
Lot or not or let's, not, go. We just went with the flow
of things there for a while. How did we know we'd end up
pure as text but not the next in any order we conceived.
The ending's only bending toward a curve, a curve a mending
coming back. Nothing we could do. How could you
conceive a narrative that simply went astray to leave
me in a book without a look at any future? What's the feature
of this portrait where I'm lit by floodlights but no moon.
Soon enough we're just the stuff of our rough sex. Six of one,
half a dozen of the other. Did you ask your mother what
she thought of this? A kiss is better than a miss, or is it now
the other way around? A pound of misery for every penny,
Sally. Sally M, that's me. You don't know how to end it,
do you? Could you bring it back to its beginning. Far too late.
The murder's been committed and the knitted scarf
is hanging on the door. Fallen on the floor. The paint is
painted over. *Or as long as men prefer to fail I'm not the*
one for judging. I'm only sorry that he now makes show
for me of unending envy. I should have said, indeed, that
in his envy there was much affection . . . Text in an archive,
live as the next thing, a pretext for making money, jumping
at the main chance. Not Maine, my love, and not Vermont,
Connecticut it is in 1962 and pro and con the island of
his birth, a near miss or near myth and did I kith you there
my tongue on trial in pages full of *plage?* Which beach
the best beat for stressed-out felon, fellow with a rhyme.
I think you'd paint my picture if it were a nude. Naked
come and naked go. I'm loath to strip my bathing suit
right off, you know. I'll do it though. The R-G voyeur
is doubtless somewhere near, his name is mine.
So also E.A.R.'s protagonist and Masolino's – fine, & in
an archive now, and in an ear. Text me a massage, oh
mesmerize me, lover & palaverer, on the tenterhooks
of ending inconclusively, although we do include herewith

a blurred photograph – the lot of you (and us) converted
into lottery. And that tuck in time's more delta than
the way it's done in dunes, a lunar kind of transcript,
transparent or opaque in which the only sense is M's
incessant murmuring about the M's's Ms. Some called it
murder, but a milder gloss held simply that the cruder
elements had now dispersed given that a deacon of
our order held the mangy Prophet by his beard.

Some Instruments for Mr. Frick

(The Winchester, the Bessemer; the Music and the Art)

Mentor Carnegie once boasted of a *permanent*
and real good to be achieved with wealth, but
only after gaining it with Henry Clay Frick through
a permanent and real harm, wooden nickels for
the hungry, and a halfpenny's humiliation
on the flip side of contempt. With a thin gloved
hand in everything, why stop short
of anything at all?
               And, as wealth accumulated,
why not gently seek to balm the tension
of an erstwhile coke-king's inner steel
by urging him to buy, while Carnegie himself
vacationed in ancestral highlands,
an Orchestrion for $6,000, lots of money then,
but still a bargain, "a good deal."
It "would give great pleasure" and would be
"A marvel there in Pittsburgh."
To the poor, the instrument became in time
a nickelodeon, a people's choir of brass
and brazen honky-tonk that all mechanically
played out the *music music music* for a time
they'd stroll the boardwalks. But as
Orchestrion, it played its pipes only for the rich,
bringing H.C.F., his colleague might well hope,
a permanent and real calm.

For he was edgy in his world of iron and
coal, his friend and partner gone out in the heather
for sabbatical. And O! The thing as advertised
could *play a gentle suite for harpsichord,*
a string serenade for nocturnal peace, even something
pastoral for shepherd's double flute. But it could
also amplify its instruments in all-Wagnerian-caboodle
with its kit of pumping bellows blazing,
its percussion rolling out the thunder for the gods.

Instead, Mr. Frick acquired some paintings – not, however
before putting down the Homestead strike, bringing
in the Pinkertons from Ashtabula – instrument
efficient in the *sturm und drang* of class warfare with
their Winchesters ablaze beyond Orchestrion's
ability to elegize the dead or trumpet either justice
or a fair wage in telegrams Carnegie might receive
in spirit of a Dutch genre sketch or a nickel for the Odeon
at some future cinema far from Skibo Castle in the rain
near Loch Rannoch.
                         By 1910 his friend's
capital conversion was complete.
So much so that Frick could bleed some assets
for a 1658 self-portrait: Chief instrument and pride
of his success: Impoverished Rembrandt,
seated like a king, his face all blasted and besmirched
as if he'd stared for thirty years into a furnace,
eyes reflected fires more lethal than a Winchester and, once
engaged, locked forever in the silent space between
collector's greed and centuries of hidden need.
No Nickelodeon, no Orchestrion to drown out the
fusillade at Homestead – just those eyes that stare, that
wounded face, the two enormous hands that look
entirely capable of anything.

V

Complayntes for Doctor Neuro

1.

Help me, music –
somehow in the way I know

       that Stefan Wolpe's music
helped his dear beloved wife
and, one brief summer, my good friend,
to live his illness with him for
a decade,   then endure . . .

I anoint myself: *What Are Winds*
And What Are Waters at my bedside
and the CD of Wolpe's violin sonata
soaring free in ecstasy, the album notes
explain, *evoking the Hassidic niggun.*

When he wrote this piece the two
of them had only met; years of love were
opening before them. Hilda's music
sings now down that dawn. It tells me
Time, memory, it's not what they say
but takes a life of its own.

       She was
across the hall from me at Yaddo
many years ago, her raw loss still new.
New poems, in pencil, appeared
under my door on crumpled spiral notebook
sheets. Anselm Hollo told me that
she'd started mourning Wolpe years before
he died. I hear her music,
and I need his own. Their music now
of grief's hope I'd borrow, but

2.

There are songs that sorrow sings:
hope's grief as sounds diabolus in scales
falling in the score and from

the eyes while Doctor Neuro says: *Just walk*
for me. Now go like this. Can you do it
faster please? Doctor Neuro says: *It's hard to tell*

at first between MG and Parkinson's. It's possible
of course to have them both. We don't do DaTscans here
that measure loss of dopamine, but serology

can turn up tags for Myasthenia. Your head is heavy
isn't it? Your arms get tired just reaching
up to brush your hair. I know. I see this frequently.

Your fingers just don't seem to work.
I sympathize: Me, I've got some nasty arthritis.
And out of nowhere then:

Do you play an instrument?

3.

You play computer screen and keyboard,
just like all those others out there in the Neuro groups.
Myasthenia is rare enough that people from

around the world seek advice and comfort from
the veterans who have known the score for years.
One poor girl writes in from Western Oz,

isolated in an outback of the mind and far
from any Neuro. She's just fourteen; she woke
one morning and she couldn't raise her

eyelids. Aristotle Onassis, Jackie's second
husband, held his up eventually with
tape. A typical first symptom, members of the

Neuro group explain. Mestinon might help. Or it
might not. She says she's just fourteen.
How long will this last?

Just one person on the listserve answers
her straight out:
This will last for your entire life.

4.

However long that is, it will be music
of some kind. Otherwise you will not dance,
my dear, even in your mind . . .

where such agility is possible for those
who only sit and wait, diatonic or octonic
as a *Man from Midian* taking first the whole steps
then the half from wheelchair on that same
program with the Aaron Copland *Billy*
whose scenario by Eugene Loring rode
the Kid & cowboys all the way to Martha Graham.

Two pianos – his and hers? – adapt a mode
that's Arabic, as Wolpe, after a short
interval, enters with the movements titled
The Procession and *Among the Workers, inter alia,*
while Copland, optimistic, oh and as American and
Prairie style as Mr. Wright, winces at wrong notes in
Taskmaster and *Restless, Desperation, Pleading.*
These four movements of the *Man from Midian*
all originating 1938, in Palestine, in polyrhythms.

A chromatic octave for your thoughts?
I think I cannot move my fingers properly,
although my poet in some future gesture of her love
will hold my hand. Does he hear her saying
east of the Black Mountain and before its time
Oh Withouten you
No leaf can blow, no bird can sing?
And later, remembering a trip to Epidaurus and
the god of healing,

Aesculapius himself,

whose shrine it was

who might have, had they stayed,
Hilda and her muse, her husband, their music,
might have whispered *Yes*

to whom at last he said, finally
from a great distance:

No.

5.

Yes, says Doctor Neuro. *I admit the situation's complicated*
and ambiguous. We have these eighteen other tests we'll
schedule, and make sure you're not unnerved by all
the ALS guys in the lobby slumped like Stephen Hawking
in their wheelchairs. None of them is wired for computer
speech, it's too expensive, and it's not covered by
the Medicare. Besides, they haven't much to say.
And don't mind the Altzies. They have lots to say of course,
though none of it makes sense. As for music, it will help.
Get yourself an iPod. You've got a favorite playlist?
Put on what you know the best, then go out and walk.
You'll find you've got more normal movement in your legs.
We don't know what explains this, and not much
else to tell the truth. The brain's a fucking
mystery. Yoga might be helpful. Try to do it wired.

And I think of their last holiday together in the south
of France. Stefan then unable to do much, but
marching off clubfooted with his poet who insists he
Sing! And down the sea cliff path they walk together,
belting out the *Marseillaise*.

6.

We drive, don't walk, even to the grocery store.
You're insecure; I'm insecure for both of us. You
Went out with a ski pole in the winter and we
Laughed about it then. You still want to use it
When it's over eighty out. I say, *just hold my arm.*
And you say, *Then I look so utterly old lady*
That it makes me laugh. Old lady me. And I say
Not so funny as a ski pole in the midsummer sun.

Is this a music? It's no *Marseillaise*. Dr. Neuro's
Ordered DaTscans in Chicago and an EMN. No one
Tells you DaTscans are for dopamine. Nor that
EMNs will stick you full of needles, Mrs. Hedgehog.
Poor old Tiggy-winkle. I'd run off and hide with you.
We'd roll up in two balls beneath that really bushy
Hedge we both remember way across the sea in
Little Shelford. There was Mrs. T, taking in the wash.

Maybe our best years, the early Seventies.
Long walks all over then. In the Gogmagogs, by the
Sea along the Suffolk coast. Now we drive a few blocks
To the supermarket, then look hard for things you'll eat.
Have they doubled stock in "health foods" just for us?
Or did we overlook it all in our good health. I vote for
Something aphrodisiac that's "bad for you": Pots of caviar,
Bottles of Merlot, a large cake called "Double Fudge."

7.

And here's the book for exercise with
Illustrations, charts. It's not just arms & legs
But neck and hips and hearts.
It's face and feet, it's eyes and ruby lips.

The voice departs just like the motions of
An art, so work on that: A, E, I, O, U.
It's Rimbaud's music of the vowels, you cows.
Look to the side, smile your wildest bride.

Stick your tongue out. Now look mad.
Now look sad and know the difference between
Sad and Angry, girl. Make it clear.
Twist and sneer. Tongue it sister if you can and

Make yourself look like a man. Sing a
Simple song. Now look long. Then look short.
Make a game of it, old sport.
Fuck you fucking with your brain. O sustain

That posture. Let it rain. Can't you rhyme it
Rain in Spain? Falls, said Higgins, *on the plain.*
Mainly, that is, Cockney Lass.
Now I kick you in the ass. If you chime it

Pain insane. Do it once and do it twice.
Can you mumble *Three Blind Mice?*
Everything's a throw of dice.
Learn each muscle has its asking price.

8.

When first I heard Stefan Wolpe's music I was
Very young — still in high school then but
Trying hard to stretch my brow
Up higher than my family's, don't you know.

Eventually, I really came to like the stuff, this
Difficult, mysterious music of a passé avant-garde.
Schoenberg, Webern, Berg, and their
Epigones. I went in earnest to their dodecophonic

School. In Columbus, string quartets performed
At intervals, rare ones like the minor sevenths, at
The art museum. I'd go there with my girlfriend
Who humored me as if my taste were even stranger

Than it was. That night in 1959 it was the Juilliard.
Webern's *Fünf Sätze*, opus 5, and Wolpe's sketches
For his still unfinished piece that Robert Mann,
His former student, had commissioned, blocked still

In his unmedicated brain. Only levodopa would
Release the rest of it, circa 1968. Having tossed
A bone to the provincial audience — early Mozart
Or a Haydn, I forget — they were poised to begin

The fragments of the quartet that they figured
Now they'd never see entire. It was a homage to
A master from his friends. Mann, the first violin,
Had explained just what they'd try to do.

Everybody held their breath and as the Juilliard
All raised their bows my girlfriend dropped her
Program on the floor. It sounded like a symbol
Crashing in Tchaikovsky. We were right in

The front row. Robert Mann turned and smiled
At poor Susan. *That's ok, my dear,* he said.
Stefan Wolpe is a sweet and understanding man.
Then we all, breathing, breathed with

The strangest sounds I'd ever heard.

9.

In my old neighborhood, there was a kid
That everybody called "Hip Hip."
He had Tourette's, though no one then had
Any sense of what that syndrome was,
Hip Hip least of all. He'd jump and twirl,
Shake his head extravagantly, then shout out
"Hip Hip and a Hershey Bar." It was a
Modest compulsion. I later knew a Tourette
Who was utterly compelled to shout out
Nigger at each passing black, appalled
At what he'd said, unable to unsay it. He was
Lucky not to have been beaten up or shot.
But Hip Hip only shouted out "Hip Hip
And a Hershey Bar." Kids these days have no
Idea what a Hershey Bar might be. We all
Got used to it, and no one thought it strange.
It's just what Hip Hip did. It was a kind
Of music. He was one of us. He too had a
Bike like all the rest. But often he'd get
Off it while we waited, spin around & throw
His arms out wide and shout: *Hip Hip
And a Hershey Bar*. It was just the thing he did.
Most of us did some weird thing.
Hip Hip. Hip. Hip Hip. Hip Hip Hip Hip.

10.

Days, there must have been, when all
The brothers and sisters afflicted
With these things were thought to be
Possessed. But by God, or by the Devil?

Or alternately first by one and then
The other. Eventually, you do get used
To using Dr. Neuro's terms: chorea,
For example. Dance, dance, twist and turn —

I brought this on her by myself through
Too much hope. What she calls "dizzy"
Is an inner turmoil like the outer one
But not observable. The mind twists

And turns, the tremors are the shakes
Of one's whole being, bradyphrenia
Occurs: Your thoughts slow down. Can
You say catechol-o-methyltransferase?

I'll bet not, but you may one day need it.
As for me, I thought an extra dose of
Sinemet might, just this once, help out.
That brought on the dyskinesias, her first

Symptoms of an overdose.
The hands twist, arms shoot out, the body
Twists and turns like . . . like . . .
Chorea, like a member of the chorus . . .

But not *quite* like that. Did I hit the chemo-
Receptive trigger zone in her brain stem?
What would they have done, our ancestors?
Set some people up as gods and goddesses?

Or from ignorance and fear, driven them from town,
Cut off their hair and tied them to a tree,
Given them examinations that they could not pass,
Or drowned them in the little lake?

11.

Good dream, good dream. Thank you
Spirits of the night. Her tormentors often
Do not spare her sleep, but last night's
Visitors did not disturb her, wreck
Her back or wrack her with the thrashing,
Make her shout out anything obscene
At all, and so I too could sleep, wrapped
Around her like an adolescent lover.

It's not that I'd been reading Ovid
Who can be as cruel in his metamorphoses
As some malign neurologist, turning
Living things into grotesques. But I feel
Certain I was visited. You'll laugh when
I tell you Zeus and Hermes were
The strangers at my door, but it is true.
Oh, of course they did not look like gods.

They looked like homeless folk, they
Looked like vagrants, like people one sees
Sleeping on the street in cardboard weather-breaks,
In old sweaters, greatcoats from the First
World War. (You'll find them there in Ovid VIII,
But I only understood that when I woke.
A gentle, generous story; rare enough and lovely
In his book. Baucis and Philemon.)

Who were my visitors? *We're fugitives,*
They sang together. But what lovely harmony!
Sounds more strange than Wolpe's, something
From another world. It was as if Abraham
And Isaac sang together walking toward an altar.

We're survivors of the war, the pogrom,
Revolution, plague, they sang. *Will you give us food?*
I said I would if only they kept singing.

I knew they were two gods in spite of what
They sang to me. *We're criminals,* they sang.
And now you must protect us, lie for us,
Offer us asylum, compromise your lives. We're ill.
How far will you go to enter our disease?
You value ease. We're here to violate all that.
We're vile, but you cannot sing yourself to being
Otherwise than by embracing us.

I pulled up wicker chairs, invited them
To sit, speared a fish with a two-tined pole from
A river that came flowing through one door
And out the other; one wall fell away revealing
Children playing by a lake our river seemed
To feed, and, three-walled only, yet the house stood
Firm and somehow firmer than it ever had before.
I found an oak leaf growing from my hand.

Goblets full of wine appeared; the oak leaf, falling,
Spread itself as tablecloth, expanding. And they sang:
Misfortune is your fortune, disorder all your order
Here. We like a house with books all over,
Manuscripts and papers in a clutter, pens leaking
Ink in pockets of discarded shirts, paintings
Hanging crooked on the wall, the wall's plaster
Cracked and open outwards for the nests of birds.

But we have never had a home ourselves
And so we ask for berries that Athena cherishes,
Endive and radishes, curdled cheese, that fish;
We ask for grapes and apples afterwards,
A comb of honey; most of all good conversation
While we eat and drink. I somehow put these

Things before them, found the fish had cooked
Although I never put it on the fire.

I asked them, were they hunted? They sang *O yes,*
By you, and also others: Stefan and Hilda,
Baucis and Philemon. By the mad who lie
On gurneys in the dark halls of institutions,
Roll in wheelchairs to groves in city parks, suck
Nutrition from the bottles full of drips that flow
Into their veins through tubes like straws they
Once shared in soda glasses with their pretty girls.

Did you know that Aesculapius arrives
In dreams as an enormous snake journeying from
Epidaurus twisted round the high mast of a ship
Summoned by us to this river by the lake? But look.
The three remaining walls of my house collapsed
And I was standing in a marble temple, and I
Was not I. Beside me, Serpent Aesculapius arose
In flaming cloak. Diana spoke: *I am a linden tree*
And what I was replied: *I have become an oak.*

Notes

Refusing an Archive
I must say a word about this poem because, in the end, I did not refuse the archive that the poem refuses. Is this hypocrisy? No, it is poetry. Following at least five years of thinking about the question, I wrote 'Refusing an Archive' at a point when I thought I had made up my mind, in part as a result of writing the poem. This may be interesting both with respect to the psychology of composition and to the integrity of the poem and its independence from the author. The poem is adamant. But I changed my mind. I see no reason for not letting the poem have its say.

Notes of an Uninvited Guest
This poem will probably make little sense to readers who do not know Thom Gunn's 'Moly,' Auden's 'In Memory of W. B. Yeats,' Robert Lowell's 'Man and Wife,' Dylan Thomas' 'Lament,' Stevens' 'Sunday Morning,' and Frost's 'Stopping by Woods on a Snowy Evening.'

In *Skunk Hour*'s Maine: Reunion at the Fosse
This poem conflates two hallucinations, both among the most uncanny experiences of my life. To be clear: After many years of being the proverbial "black sheep" in my family, despite the fact that only I and my daughters retain the family name, I returned to a reunion at a cousin's summer house in Maine. Not having seen any of these relatives for many years, I was fully conscious of seeing my dead parents among them when I opened the door. They were there, then vanished. I cannot explain this. Many years before, my elder daughter, Cynouai, confused my father's oldest friend for my father himself at his funeral. I do not think this poem is adequate to these events, but it has been so far the best that I can do.

Song of the Association's Spokesman
I am no friend of the National Rifle Association, nor of its president Wayne LaPierre. The poem is based on a famous one in Portuguese by Carlos Drummond de Andrade, 'In the Middle of the Road.' The translation below is by Mark Strand. To press associations from one language through another and back to English, I like it that "stone" in French is *la pierre*.

In the Middle of the Road

In the middle of the road there was a stone
There was a stone in the middle of the road
There was a stone
In the middle of the road there was a stone.

I'll never forget this event
In the lifetime of my tired eyes.
I'll never forget that in the middle of the road
There was a stone
There was a stone in the middle of the road
In the middle of the road there was a stone.

After *Las Formas Puras*, after Lorca

This poem is even less a 'proper' translation than the Quevedo version that follows it. It is dedicated to the memory of Anthony Kerrigan because Tony and I used to kill the time now and then doing what he called, after Lorca, some *hechos poéticos*, slowly improvised riffs or improvisations in which we'd feed each other a line from a text and the other would do something with it and then toss it back — which is not, by the way, what Lorca meant by the term. Anthony Kerrigan, of course, was one of the great Spanish language translators of the twentieth century who played these games with me now and then to amuse himself. We were down the hallway from each other at Notre Dame for about a decade. When I found 'After *Las Formas Puras*, after Lorca' in an old notebook recently, I realized that it derived from the *hechos* game with Tony some twenty years ago. I discovered its actual source in the last stanza of the third poem in Lorca's *Poeta en Nueva York*, one of the 'Poems of Solitude at Columbia University': 'Fábula y rueda de los tres amigos,' or 'Fable of Three Friends to Be Sung in Rounds.' Only a few of the last twelve lines of the 'Fable' are consecutively translated, and other lines are either imported from other Lorca poems or inventions based on Lorca's words and phrases. Still, my working definition of 'translation' is as broad as I can make it, and so by a stretch this *hecho*-derived poem belongs in a group of translations rather than a group of original poems. The most useful thing I can do for the reader is to print below the twelve Lorca lines at issue, and follow them with a pretty literal English version in the excellent Greg Simon/Steven F. White translation (*Poet in New York*, Noonday Press, 1988).

Cuando se hundieron las formas puras
bajo el cri cri de las margaritas,

comprendí que me habían asesinado.
Recorrieron los cafés y los cementerios y las iglesias.
Abrieron los toneles y los armarios.
Destrozaron tres esqueletos para arrancar sus dientes de oro.
Y no me encontraron.
¿No me encontraron?
Pero se supo que la sexta luna huyó torrente arriba,
y que el mar recordó ¡de pronto!
los nombres de todos sus ahogados.

"When the pure shapes sank / under the chirping of daisies,/ I knew they had murdered me. / They combed the cafés, graveyards, and churches for me, / pried open casks and cabinets, / destroyed three skeletons in order to rip out their gold teeth. / But they couldn't find me anymore. / They couldn't? / No, they couldn't find me. / But they discovered the sixth moon had fled against the torrent, / and the sea – suddenly! – remembered / the names of all its drowned."

After Quevedo

This is more of a trespass than a translation of Quevedo's 'Amor constanta más allá de la muerte.' I am by no means a Quevedo scholar and even my knowledge of Spanish is rusty enough to require assistance from existing translations and commentaries. My English version is not, as will be immediately obvious to anyone who knows the original, a literal translation. More than that, the initial inspiration to work with the text was indirect rather than direct. A while ago I wrote an essay called 'Grand Old Dirty Old Men,' which now appears in *Who Was Cousin Alice? And Other Questions*, a hybrid volume of memoirs, essays, and poems. I ended that piece with a reading of two late books by Octavio Paz, *The Double Flame: Love and Eroticism* and *An Erotic Beyond: Sade*. Late in his life, Paz was haunted by Quevedo's baroque masterpiece, 'Amor constanta más allá de la muerte.' Paz finds Quevedo breaking with both Christianity and Platonism in his poem, and in fact 'violating' both traditions in a kind of double heresy. Readers not familiar with Spanish Baroque poetry may initially think of John Donne when encountering the poem for the first time. But it is perhaps more radical than anything in Donne. Calling the poem blasphemous, Paz is in fact thrilled as well as unnerved by the imagery of mortal desire lasting beyond death and finds Quevedo's poem to be itself the urn containing immortal remains still with mortal longings: 'Although the body deteriorates into formless matter, the matter is animate. The power that animates it and imbues it with a terrible eternity is love, desire.' My version mixes the dust of the beloved with that of the lover in that urn, and it retains fragments or the original "matter" of the Spanish like tiny pieces of bone in the ash.

The second source of my own fascination with the poem is much more distant. Ever since I was a student of Yvor Winters, I have found two of his poems, 'The Marriage' and 'The Cremation,' as haunting as Paz finds 'Amor constanta más allá de la muerte.' Winters knew the Spanish Baroque tradition well, and he made some translations from its canon of great poems. Here is the end of 'The Marriage':

> When flesh shall fall away, and, falling, stand
> Wrinkling with shadow over face and hand,
> Still I shall meet you on the verge of dust
> And know you as a faithful visage must
> And, in commemoration of our lust,
> May our heirs seal us in a single urn,
> A single spirit never to return.

But the two dusts in my Quevedo version do not reduce to 'a single spirit' because it is not 'lust' that is being 'commemorated,' but 'Amor constanta' [constant love] 'más allá de la muerte' [even beyond death] that is being celebrated, and in a way that should appall even as it stimulates the imagination of a reader who might perhaps have fed on Baudelaire or Poe. That reader must actually try to see the convergence, the movement of the particles in the urn as they grope toward each other. Only a baroque style, it seems to me, can achieve this, and I have exaggerated the tortuousness of that style in my homage, which, again, is also a trespass. Winters' 'The Cremation' asks, in its middle stanza, 'And where is that which made you just? / Which gathered light about the bone / And moved the tongue, in earth's despite?' In Quevedo it is all there in the urn, and preternaturally alive.

The M's's
The conclusion of this poem as originally printed included the following note under the heading of 'His Glass as Gloss': M, his lot: *Acts* 1/26; M, his portrait: Masolino, 1428; M, his tale: Robinson, 1931; M as voyeur: Robbe-Grillet, 1958; M, as mistress: Updike, 1976; M, his kingdom: Johnson and Wilentz, 1994; M, his archive: Cooley, 1998; M, his madness, 2014 ff. That in itself was intended to be an oblique statement on method. However, I can extend that here by noting that most of us are at least momentarily surprised when we see our own name in a printed text — especially, perhaps, in fiction. In my case, this surprise dates from my childhood when I first read Acts I.26 about the lot falling on Matthias. My father used to take his oath

of office (Supreme Court of Ohio) with his hand on that passage. When I first encountered the neurophysicist and contemporary composer John Matthias in print, I was led to incorporate his work in a book-length poem called *Trigons*. I also eventually corresponded with this other John Matthias and met him for lunch. 'The M's's' derives from seven sources dealing with a protagonist called Matthias or Mathias. The plots are extrapolated and braided, leading to yet other plots. One source, the Masolino 'St. Matthias and the Pope,' is a painting rather than a text. Nobody reads E. A. Robinson's narrative poems any longer, but one of them is called 'Matthias at the Door.' The Updike novel in question is *Marry Me*; Martha Cooley's Matthias is an archivist; Robbe-Grillet's is a voyeur. Paul E. Johnson and Sean Wilentz tell the strange story of *The Kingdom of Matthias: Sex and Salvation in 19th-Century America*. My title, of course, besides referencing all of these figures with the same surname, is at some points also ambiguously hovering between a feminine Ms. — 'for M is also female' — and the abbreviation for the manuscript(s), Ms and Mss, she morphs into and emerges out of, like M himself.

Complayntes for Doctor Neuro. A Poetics of Parkinson's

(*Complaynt:* Late Middle English, from Old French *complaynte,* from *com-plaindre,* 'to lament'). The cycle of poems called 'Complayntes for Doctor Neuro' is also, of course, an extended love poem for my wife, Diana. When any marriage is invaded by an insidious progressive illness, from that time on it is a marriage of three. I've known some people to give their conditions nicknames, and I understand why. The invading third party is always just around the corner, and one feels like calling it something nasty when trying to chase it away with a stick, a broom, a drug. I do not have Parkinson's myself, but when my wife was finally diagnosed some years ago, after having been misdiagnosed, I had to become an expert. I have an entire library of neurological books, half of them with a Parkinson's focus.

My 'complaynte,' which I spell with an 'e,' as some medieval and sixteenth-century poets did, when complaining to their mistresses in poems, should be understood as a response to dealing with the earliest and most mysterious manifestations of the condition and its treatment. A common experience of patients is misdiagnosis — and we had to deal with that at first. There are a large number of neurological conditions with initial symptoms similar to Parkinson's, and one of those can be Myasthenia Gravis. Diana was at first told that she had MG and began taking the standard medication for that condition called Mestinon, an anti-acetylcholinesterase agent, which allows acetylcholine to remain at the neuromuscular junction longer than usual so that more receptor sites can be activated. Strangely, it seemed at first to work, so the initial sections of my poem wander back and forth from Myasthenia Gravis to other possible conditions. All patients with rare conditions crave communication with others who are experiencing their symptoms, and my wife and I spent long periods with Internet groups for MG until one of them suggested that Diana should be tested for Parkinson's.

There is, of course, no "test" for Parkinson's as there is for MG, so we ended up at the University of Chicago after a year or so where our third neurologist made the tentative diagnosis, eliminated MG (it is actually possible to have both conditions), and began prescribing levodopa, the correct initial medication if one has doubts, as we did, regarding the possible bad side effects of the class of drugs known as Agonists. Eventually, Parkinson's patients are likely to add Agonists and other classes of drugs to the levodopa supplementation, but not necessarily for several years. One of the first things that the inexperienced are likely to do is to overdose on levodopa, as the drug makes one feel better very quickly. This will bring on dyskinesia and chorea, frightening both the patient and the person trying to help (and who, as in my own case, may have encouraged the overdosing). Dyskinesia is the opposite of dystonia, which is the "frozen" symptom caused by the illness itself, not by the drug used to treat it. Among all of the books I have read, I would most recommend two by J. Eric Ahlskog of the Mayo Clinic: *The Parkinson's Disease Treatment Book: Partnering with Your Doctor to Get the Most from Your Medications*, and its companion volume for physicians, *Parkinson's Disease Treatment Guide for Physicians.*

Luckily, I was not entirely ignorant of the neurology I had to begin learning better. My uncle, Edward Matthias, was a veteran of World War I and one of the first to contract the post-war Spanish Influenza and the side effects that were, in his case, untreatable. It was only when Oliver Sacks began giving levodopa to his patients with post–Spanish flu Parkinsonian symptoms called *encephalitis lethargica*, or sleeping sickness, that the revolution in treatment of PD itself began. If you have read Sacks' *Awakenings*, or seen the excellent film made from the book, you will recognize both dystonia and dyskinesia. The later looks bad but, within reason, feels good. The former left my uncle frozen in his chair for twenty years and more. Having been as a child somewhat morbidly fascinated by my uncle's condition, I read up on the post-war flu and its aftermath. When *Awakenings* was published in 1973 it was a revelation.

Over the years, levodopa treatments (now combined with carbidopa) have been carefully titrated. If one is a smart patient, one begins very quickly to vary medication a bit from day to day, and even through a day, to correspond with how one is feeling. Diana and I have often modified our neurologists' instructions. You begin by wanting every small change to be approved, but waiting for phone calls or email returns gets in the way of following the advice of major researchers like Dr. Ahlskog in good time. If anyone reading these notes is confronting Parkinson's, my most urgent advice is simple: Learn all you possibly can.

My poem begins as a kind of dialogue with one of my favorite poets, Hilda Morley. I met Hilda at the Yaddo artists' colony in 1982, I believe, a year or so before she published her poems written to and about her husband, Stefan Wolpe, the composer, published in *What Are Winds and What Are Waters*. I already knew and admired Wolpe's music, so I was delighted to meet Hilda. What I didn't know was that Hilda had nursed Wolpe through his Parkinson's for a decade and more before the life-changing levodopa became available to patients. Her poems to Wolpe, which are marvelous, became permission, as Robert Duncan would have said, to write my own. The writing itself was often accompanied by Wolpe CDs — the *String Quartet*, *The Man from Midian*, and the *Sonata for Violin and Piano*. One of the poems describes my youthful experience of hearing the *String Quartet*, performed by the Juilliard Quartet, before it was finished — though finished it later was, thanks to the drugs that finally became available to the composer, including levodopa. In those days — I was not yet eighteen — I wonder what I thought I was hearing, not to say what it all prefigured. Hilda Morley called her Collected Poems *Cloudless at First*, and so it is for most of us. But the heavy weather will come.

Lightning Source UK Ltd.
Milton Keynes UK
UKOW02f1423230816

281322UK00001B/91/P